The Cambridge Manuals of Science and
Literature

THE GROUND PLAN OF THE
ENGLISH PARISH CHURCH

Hedon, Yorkshire : nave from N.W.

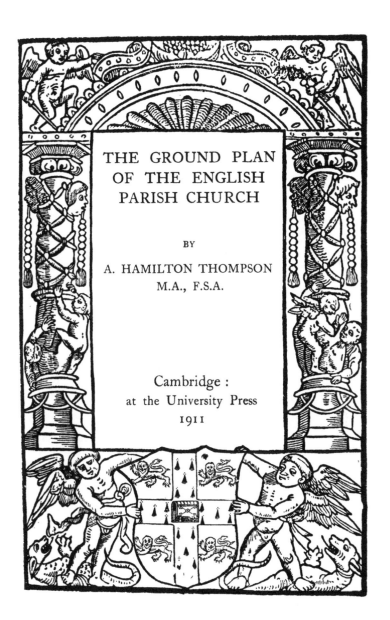

THE GROUND PLAN
OF THE ENGLISH
PARISH CHURCH

BY

A. HAMILTON THOMPSON
M.A., F.S.A.

Cambridge :
at the University Press
1911

CAMBRIDGE UNIVERSITY PRESS
Cambridge, New York, Melbourne, Madrid, Cape Town,
Singapore, São Paulo, Delhi, Tokyo, Mexico City

Cambridge University Press
The Edinburgh Building, Cambridge CB2 8RU, UK

Published in the United States of America by
Cambridge University Press, New York

www.cambridge.org
Information on this title: www.cambridge.org/9781107401600

First published 1911
First paperback edition 2011

A catalogue record for this publication is available from the British Library

ISBN 978-1-107-40160-0 Paperback

*With the exception of the coat of arms
at the foot, the design on the title page is a
reproduction of one used by the earliest known
Cambridge printer, John Siberch, 1521*

PREFACE

THERE is as yet no book entirely devoted to the development of the plan of the parish church in England, and the body of literature which bears upon the subject is not very accessible to the ordinary student. The present volume is an attempt to indicate the main lines on which that development proceeded. It is obvious that, from necessary considerations of space, much has been omitted. The elevation of the building, and the treatment of its decorative features, window-tracery, sculpture, etc., belong to another and wider branch of architectural study, in which the parish church pursues the same line of structural development as the cathedral or monastic church, and the architectural forms of the timber-roofed building follow the example set by the larger churches with their roofs of stone. To this side of the question much attention has been devoted, and of late years increasing emphasis has been laid on the importance of the vaulted construction of our greater churches, which is the very foundation of medieval architecture and the secret of its progress through its various "styles." It is expected that the reader of this book, in which a less familiar but none the less important topic is handled, will already have some acquaintance with the general progress of medieval architectural forms, with which the development of the ground plan keeps pace.

Some historical and architectural questions, which arise out of the consideration of the ground plan, and have an important bearing upon it, are treated in another volume of this series, which is intended to be complementary to the present one.

The writer is grateful to his wife, for the plans and sketches which she has drawn for him, and for much help ; to Mr C. C. Hodges and Mr J. P. Gibson, for the permission to make use of their photographs ; and to the Rev. J. C. Cox, LL.D., F.S.A., and the Rev. R. M. Serjeantson, M.A., F.S.A., for their kindness in reading through the proofs and supplying suggestions of the greatest value.

A. H. T.

GRETTON, NORTHANTS
26 *January* 1911

CONTENTS

CHAPTER I

THE ORIGIN OF THE CHURCH PLAN IN ENGLAND

CHAPTER II

PARISH CHURCHES OF THE LATER SAXON PERIOD

CHAPTER III

THE AISLELESS CHURCH OF THE NORMAN PERIOD

CHAPTER IV

THE AISLED PARISH CHURCH

I.   NAVE, TOWER, AND PORCHES

CHAPTER V

THE AISLED PARISH CHURCH

II.   TRANSEPTS AND CHANCEL

CONTENTS

LIST OF ILLUSTRATIONS

CHAPTER I

§ 1. Side by side with the establishment of Christianity as the religion of the Roman empire, there appeared a fully developed plan for places of Christian worship. The normal Christian church of the fourth century of our era was an aisled building with the entrance at one end, and a semi-circular projection known as the apse at the other. The body of the building, the nave with its aisles, was used by the congregation, the quire of singers occupying a space, enclosed within low walls, at the end nearest the apse. In the apse, raised above the level of the nave, was the altar, behind which, ranged round the wall, were the seats for the bishop and assistant clergy. This type of church, of which the aisled nave and the apse are the essential parts, is known as the *basilica*. The name, employed to designate a "royal" or magnificent building, had long been applied to large buildings, whether open to the sky or roofed, which were used, partly as commercial exchanges, partly as halls of justice. It is still often said that the Christian basilicas were merely adaptations of such buildings to sacred purposes. Some of the features of the Christian plan are akin to those of the secular basilica. The apse with its semi-circular range of seats and its altar reproduces the judicial tribune, with its seats for the praetor and his assistant judges, and its altar on which oaths were taken. The open galleries, which in some of the earliest Christian basilicas at Rome form an upper story to the aisles, recall the galleries above the colonnades which surrounded the central hall of some of the larger secular basilicas. Again, the *atrium* or forecourt through which the Christian basilica was often approached has been supposed to be derived from the *forum* in connexion with which the secular basilica was frequently built.

§ 2. However, while the *atrium* of the Christian basilica is merely an outer court, the secular basilica, when planned, like the Basilica Ulpia at Rome, with direct relation to a *forum*, was a principal building in connexion with the *forum*, but not a building of which the *forum* was a mere annexe. Further, when we begin to seek for a complete identification of the Christian with the secular basilica, we are met by the obstacle that the secular basilica had no fixed plan. If we try to trace any principle of development in its plan, we find that this develop-

ment is directly inverse to that of the Christian
basilica. The secular basilica, in earlier examples
a colonnaded building with its central space open to
the sky, became at a later time a roofed hall, either,
as in the case of the basilica at Trier, without aisles,
or, like the basilica of Maxentius or Constantine in
the Roman forum, with a series of deep recesses at
the side, the vaulted roofs of which served to counter-
act the outward pressure of the main vault. The
Christian basilica, if it were a mere imitation of this
type of building, would follow the same line of development ; but, as a matter of fact, the highest type
of Christian church is always a colonnaded or aisled
building. And, even if the Christian apse derived
its arrangement from the apse or apses which projected from the ends or sides of the secular basilicas,
there is again a difference. The apse with its altar
was the main feature of the interior of the Christian
church : it was the place in which the chief rite of
Christian worship was performed before the eyes of all.
In the secular basilica the apse was devoted to special
purposes which set it apart from the main business of
the body of the building : it was an appendage to the
central hall, not necessarily within view of every part
of it. In fact, the relation of the apse to the main
building was totally different in the two cases.

§ 3. It seems probable, then, that the identity
between the two buildings is mainly an identity of

name, and that Christian builders, in seeking for suitable arrangements for public worship, may have borrowed some details from the arrangements of the secular basilica. It is natural, however, to look for the origin of a religious plan in buildings devoted to religious purposes. The Roman temple supplied no help for the plan of buildings which were required for public worship. Of recent years, it has been customary to assume that the Christian basilica took its form from the inner halls of the private houses of those wealthy citizens who embraced Christianity in its early days. Such halls may have been used for Christian services; and if their plan was adopted for the Christian basilica, the mature state of the basilican plan at its first appearance can be explained. The *atrium* or entrance hall of the house is represented on this hypothesis by the forecourt of the basilica; the peristyle, or colonnade round the inner room, becomes the aisles and the space screened off at the entrance for those not entitled to take full part in the service; the colonnade at the further end survives in the arcaded screen which existed, for example, in old St Peter's at Rome; the apse takes the place of the *tablinum*, where the most sacred relics of family life were preserved; and the transept, which is found in some of the early Roman basilican plans, represents the *alae*, or transverse space, which existed between the *tablinum* and the main body of the

hall. But these close analogies are the result of an
assumption by no means certain. It is always probable
that the basilican plan had its origin in a plan originally aisleless. Some, intent on its religious source,
explain it as a development of the plan of the Jewish
synagogue. Others, regarding assemblies of Chris-
tians for public worship as, in their essence, meetings
of persons associated in common brotherhood, have
derived the basilica directly from the aisleless *scholae*
which were the meeting-places of the various confra-
ternities or *collegia* of ancient Rome. In these there
is an apse at one end of the building; and, if we
imagine aisles added by the piercing of the walls with
rows of arches and columns, we have at once the
essential features of the basilican plan. Each theory
has its attractions and its difficulties; and to none is
it possible to give unqualified adherence. It may be
stated, as a tentative conclusion, that the basilican
plan probably had its origin in an aisleless form of
building, and thus pursued a course directly opposite
to the development of the secular basilica. But it
seems clear that, in many details of the plan, especially
as we see it in Rome, the peristyled hall was kept in
mind; while in two features, the arrangement of the
apse and the occasional appearance of galleries above
the aisles, the secular basilica was taken into consideration. The policy of the early Christian Church,
when its services were sanctioned by the state, was

to adapt existing and familiar forms where they could be suitably reproduced.

§ 4. The plan of the old basilica of St Peter at Rome, founded by Constantine the Great, and destroyed early in the sixteenth century to make way for the present church, explains the principal features of the basilican plan in its developed state. (1) In common with other early basilicas in Rome, and in

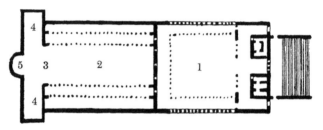

Fig. 1. Plan of old St Peter's: (1) *atrium* or fore-court; (2) nave with double aisles; (3) site of screen-colonnade; (4, 4) transepts; (5) apse with crypt below.

other parts of western Europe, the entrance was at the east, and the altar at the west end, so that the celebrant faced the congregation during the divine office. (2) The church was approached through a cloistered *atrium* or fore-court, in the middle of which was a fountain, the place of purification for those intending to enter the church. (3) At the west end of the cloister three doorways opened into the nave of the church, and one on either side into the side aisles. (4) The nave communicated with the aisles by a row of columns beneath an entablature : there were also outer aisles, communicating with the inner by columns bearing rounded arches. (5) The side walls of the nave, above the entablature, were not pierced for galleries, but were covered by two rows of mosaic pictures, one above the other, on each side, the upper row corresponding to the height of the space between the outer and inner roofs of the aisle. Above this, the walls rose into a clerestory, pierced with round-headed windows at regular intervals ; and a high entablature supported the great tie-beams of the wooden roof. (6) The quire of singers, divided from the rest of the church by low screen walls, probably occupied the centre of the western portion of the nave. (7) A tall open arch divided the nave from the transept, which was of equal height with the nave, and projected south and north as far as the walls of the outer aisles. Here probably were places reserved for distinguished persons, near the platform of the altar. (8) West of the transept, entered by a tall and wide arch, was the apse. Beneath the arch was a screen, formed by a row of columns, under an entablature which bore statues of our Lord and the apostles : this crossed the arch at the foot of the steps leading to the altar and seats of the clergy. (9) Beneath the altar plat-

form, and entered by doorways on each side of the
flight of steps, was the crypt or *confessio*, the traditional place of martyrdom of St Peter, and the
resort of pilgrims to the tomb of the apostles.   The
hallowed place was immediately beneath the altar.

§ 5.   The sixth century basilicas of Ravenna, Sant'
Apollinare in Classe and Sant' Apollinare Nuovo,
differ in plan from the Roman basilicas (1) in the fact
that they have always had the altar at the east, and
the entrance at the west end ; (2) by substituting, for
a colonnaded atrium, a closed porch or *narthex* in
front of the entrance of the building.   In process of
time, two of the greater Roman basilicas, San Paolo
and San Lorenzo fuori le Mura, were enlarged in
a westward direction, so that the positions of the
altar and entrance were reversed ; and, in several of
the early basilicas at Rome, a space near the entrance
of the nave was screened off, from which penitents
and catechumens might watch the service.   But, in
the first instance, the eastern chancel and the structural *narthex* appear to have been introduced from
the eastern empire.   Neither at Ravenna nor at
Rome did bell-towers originally form part of the
plan of the basilica : the round *campanili* of both
churches at Ravenna are certainly later additions.   It
may also be noted (1) that ordinarily the aisles were
single, not double as at old St Peter's.   (2) The
columned screen of the apse at old St Peter's ap-

pears to have been exceptional. The ordinary screen
or *cancelli*, from which is derived our word "chancel"
for the space thus enclosed, was a low wall. This is
the arrangement at the basilica of San Clemente, in
which the enclosed quire also remains. (3) The
transept, even in Rome, was an exceptional arrangement, and does not appear in the basilicas of Ravenna.

§ 6. Another type of plan, however, was used in
Rome for churches devoted to the special purposes
of burial and baptism. In this case the buildings
were planned round a central point, and at Rome
were uniformly circular. Recesses round the walls of
the mausoleum-church contained sarcophagi: in the
centre of the baptistery was the great font. The church
of Santa Costanza, outside the north-eastern walls of
Rome, circular in plan, with a vaulted aisle surround-
ing the central space, was built by Constantine the
Great as a tomb-church for his family, and was also
used as a baptistery. Both these uses were direct
adaptations of pagan customs. The baptistery, with
its central font for total immersion, was simply a large
bath-room, like the great rotunda of the baths of
Caracalla. The mausoleum preserved the form of
which the finest example is the tomb of Hadrian,
now known as the castle of Sant' Angelo. In the
course of the middle ages, certain tomb-churches in
Rome, with a centralised plan, were turned into places
of public worship. But, for the plan of the ordinary

church, the basilica, with its longitudinal axis, was general. In the eastern empire, on the other hand, the centralised plan was employed from an early date for large churches ; and in this way was evolved the magnificent style of architecture which culminated in Santa Sophia at Constantinople. Here the centralised plan was triumphantly adapted to the internal arrangements of the basilica.

§ 7. The city of Ravenna, closely connected historically both with Rome and Constantinople, contains a series of monuments which is of unequalled interest in the history of the centralised plan. (1) The mausoleum of the empress Galla Placidia, sister of the emperor Honorius, who died in 450 A.D., is a building of cruciform shape, consisting of a square central space covered by a dome, with rectangular projections on all four sides. The projection through which the building is entered is longer than the others, and the plan thus forms the Latin cross so common in the churches of the middle ages. (2) To the same period belongs the octagonal baptistery, known as San Giovanni in Fonte. (3) In 493 A.D. Theodoric the Ostrogoth obtained possession of Ravenna. To the period of his rule belongs the Arian baptistery, also octagonal, known as Santa Maria in Cosmedin. (4) Theodoric died in 526 A.D. His mausoleum is formed by a polygon of ten equal sides, with a smaller decagonal upper stage, a circular attic above

which bears the great monolithic dome.   In the lower
story was the tomb: the internal plan is a Greek
cross, *i.e.* there is a central space with recesses of

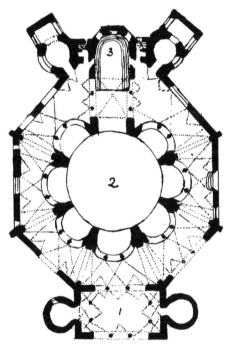

Fig. 2. Plan of San Vitale, Ravenna: (1) *narthex* with flanking
turrets, as originally arranged; (2) central nave; (3) chancel
and altar.

equal depth on all four sides. (5) In the year of the
death of Theodoric, the octagonal church of San
Vitale was begun. It was consecrated in 547, when
Ravenna had become the capital of the Italian
province of Justinian's empire. Its somewhat complicated plan was clearly derived from an eastern
source, but not from Santa Sophia, which was not
begun till 532 A.D. The central space is almost
circular. Between each of the piers which support
the octagonal clerestory at the base of the cupola is
an apsidal recess, with three arches on the ground
floor opening into the encircling aisle, and three upper
arches opening into the gallery above the aisle. On
the east side of the central space this arrangement is
broken, and one tall arch opens into the chancel,
which ends in a projecting apse, semi-circular inside,
but a half octagon outside. The aisle with the gallery
above thus occupies seven sides of the outer octagon,
the eighth side being occupied by the western part of
the chancel.

§ 8. Of the two types of plan, which can be
studied so satisfactorily at Ravenna, the ordinary
basilican type is the more convenient. The long nave
provides the necessary accommodation for worship-
pers, the raised apse gives a theatre for the perform-
ance of service within view of everybody, the aisles
facilitate the going and coming of the congregation,
and prevent over-crowding. The centralised plan

provides, it is true, a large central area conveniently
near the altar; but the provision of a chancel or
altar-space necessitates the grafting on the plan of a
feature borrowed from the ordinary basilica, which,
as at San Vitale, breaks the symmetry of the design.
At Santa Sophia, the basilican chancel forms an in-
dissoluble part of a centralised plan; but this feat is
beyond the reach of an ordinary architect. Even at
San Vitale the planning is highly complicated, and
must be due to an architect of some genius. In
addition to complications of design, the centralised
plan raised questions of roofing which did not trouble
the builders of the long wooden-roofed basilicas. The
vaulted half-dome of the basilican apse was a simple
matter, compared with the mighty dome of Santa
Sophia and its cluster of abutting half-domes. It was
in the centralised churches, with their domed vaults
and the groined vaults of their aisles, that the history
of medieval vaulting began. But, even when medieval
masons had learned to regard the vaulting of their
churches as the controlling principle of their art,
they left the centralised plan almost entirely alone,
and applied what it had taught them to the work of
roofing basilicas with vaults of stone. We shall trace
the influence of the centralised church as we proceed;
but the influence of the basilica will be found to pre-
dominate in the history of medieval planning.

§ 9. In England, as in other portions of the

Roman empire, we might naturally expect to find
the basilican plan applied to the earliest Christian
churches. The foundations of a small Romano-British
basilican church have been discovered at Silchester in
Hampshire. The apse, as in the Roman basilicas, was
at the west end. The nave had aisles, which, at the
end nearest the apse, broadened out into two transept-
like projections. The entrance front of the church
was covered by a *narthex*, the whole width of nave
and aisles. This feature, as has been shown, is of
eastern rather than of Roman origin ; while the projections at the end of the aisles appear to have been,
not transepts like those at old St Peter's, but separate
chambers corresponding to those which, in eastern
churches, flank the chancel, and are used for special
ritual purposes. In fact, the basilica at Silchester
recalls the plans of the early basilicas of north Africa
more closely than those of the basilicas of Rome ;
while it has, unlike them, the Roman feature of the
western apse. This, however, gives rise to questions
which, in our present state of knowledge, are beyond
solution.

§ 10. Of the seven churches which are usually
connected with the missionary activity of St Augustine
and his companions, five, of which we have ruins or
foundations, certainly ended in apses; and the apse in
each case was divided from the nave, not by a single
arch, but by an arcade with three openings, which

recalls the screen-colonnade at old St Peter's. But
only one church in the group, the ruined church of
Reculver, followed the plan of the aisled nave of the
basilica. From the description which remains of the
early cathedral of Canterbury, destroyed by fire in
1067, we can see that it, too, was an aisled basilica,
with its original apse at the west end. But the first
cathedral of Rochester, the plan and extent of which
may be gathered from existing foundations, was an
aisleless building with an eastern apse. The church
of St Pancras at Canterbury, the lower courses of
the walls of which in great part remain, had an
aisleless nave, divided from an apsidal chancel by a
screen-wall with three openings, that in the middle
being wider than the others. The foundations of
two of the four columns which flanked these openings
can still be traced. The walls of the chancel, which
was slightly narrower than the nave, were continued
straight for a little way beyond the screen-wall ;
and then the curve of the apse began. St Pancras
also possessed a square entrance porch, much narrower
than the nave, at its west end, and two chapels
projecting from the nave on either side, half-way
up its length. The church is thus cruciform in
plan. The western porch and the chapels seem to
have been added as the work proceeded, and not
to have been contemplated in the original design.
The material of the building is Roman brick, and

buttress projections occur at the western angles of
the nave and porch, in the fragment which remains
of the south wall of the chancel, and at the outer
angles of the side chapels.   Small buttresses are also
found at the angles and on the sides of St Peter's on
the Wall in Essex.

§ 11.   In one respect the plan of St Pancras at
Canterbury is allied to that of the church at Bradford-
on-Avon in Wiltshire.   At Bradford there remains
one of the two porches, which also were probably side
chapels, projecting from the sides of the nave.   But
at Bradford the remaining porch is larger in proportion to the nave than is the case at St Pancras.
There is no entrance porch on the west side.   Further,
the chancel at Bradford is rectangular, not apsidal.
Instead of a screen-wall with a central opening nine
feet wide, the wall dividing nave from chancel is
pierced by a small arch only 3 ft. 6 in. wide.   The date
of this little church is a matter of great difficulty ;
and the character of its masonry seems to demand
for it a later date than the early one popularly claimed
for it.   The contrast with St Pancras is accentuated
further by the fact that the internal measurements of
the nave show a different scheme of proportion.   The
nave of St Pancras is some three feet broader in proportion to its length than the much shorter nave at
Bradford.

§ 12.   A closer parallel to Bradford-on-Avon is

found in the little church of Escomb, near Bishop Auckland. No record of the early history of this building is known ; but its masonry is almost entirely composed of re-used Roman dressed stone-work. In this respect it presents a contrast to Bradford. In another respect the two churches are unlike. Both have their entrances in the side walls ; but at Escomb there were no original porches covering the doorways, while there are traces of what may have been an entrance porch, like that of St Pancras, at the west

Fig. 3. Plan of Escomb—typical Saxon church.

end. But they have these points in common : (1) the nave at Escomb is long in proportion to its width ; (2) the chancel is a rectangular eastern projection, narrower and much shorter than the nave ; (3) there is a solid wall of division between nave and chancel, pierced by a narrow arch, broader than that of Bradford, but very much higher in proportion to its width. It may be added that the walls of both churches are high in proportion to their length and breadth, and that at Escomb the original windows are small openings with rounded and flat lintel-heads, and with internal splays.

§ 13. It is, however, with the plan that we are concerned. We now have met with three separate forms in England, viz. (1) the rare basilican plan; (2) the "Kentish" plan of aisleless nave with apsidal chancel; (3) the plan of aisleless nave with rectangular chancel. We also have seen that the screen-wall is common to (1) and (2), while the single chancel arch belongs to (3); and that side chapels and western porches are found incidentally in (2) and (3). Now, the early date of Escomb, apart from the evidence supplied by its masonry, can be suspected only by its analogy to the plan of other churches of which the date is practically certain. Two such churches remain in the same county of Durham. One is at Monkwearmouth, now a part of Sunderland. Its nave and the lowest stage of its western tower represent, and in great part actually are, the nave and western porch of an early Saxon church, which is generally identified with the church built here by Benedict Biscop for the monastery which he founded in 672 A.D. The nave was originally aisleless, long, narrow and lofty: the entrance porch had an upper story finished with a gabled roof, and a vaulted ground-floor with entrances on three sides. There was evidently a chancel arch, and probably the chancel was rectangular. The material of the building was not Roman ; but, in the decoration applied to it, Roman work was imitated. Only a few miles further north, Benedict founded, in 680 A.D., the sister monastery of Jarrow. The long and narrow chancel of the present church of St Paul was the body of a church somewhat similar to that of Monkwearmouth. Stone-work which may represent the jambs of a broad chancel arch can be traced in the east wall ; but this cannot be stated with positive certainty. The lower part of the tower, now between the present chancel and nave, may represent an original western porch; but, in its present state, it is of much later date than the work east of it, and its site must have been broadened when the tower was first planned. At Jarrow there is no Roman stone-work ; but one type of Roman masonry has been imitated by the builders in the walls of the chancel, and small decorative shafts, turned in a lathe after the Roman fashion, such as exist at Monkwearmouth, have been found in the building. The inscribed stone, recording the dedication of the church, is preserved in the wall above the western tower-arch : the date given is 23 April, 684 A.D. In this inscription the building, though aisleless, is called a basilica. The word was now probably used to signify a Christian church, irrespective of its plan. A third early church in this district is that of Corbridge, near Hexham. Here, as at Monkwearmouth, the ground story of the tower was originally a western porch ; while the lofty arch between tower and nave is, like the chancel arch at Escomb, entirely composed of dressed Roman masonry, and seems to have been removed from one of the buildings of the Roman station of Corstopitum, as the arch at Escomb was probably removed from the not far distant station of Vinovium.

§ 14. The date to which these four northern churches may be assigned is the half century of the activity of St Wilfrid in England (664–709 A.D.). Bede's account of the architectural work of Wilfrid's friend, Benedict Biscop, shows that he procured, for the building of the church at Monkwearmouth, stonemasons and glaziers from Gaul, who were acquainted with "the manner of the Romans." The account which another contemporary, Eddius, gives of Wilfrid's church at Hexham, is clear proof that this important building was a reproduction, in plan and elevation, of the aisled basilicas of the continent— a fact in keeping with Wilfrid's life-long aim of bringing English Christianity into closer touch with the main current of historic Christianity in Rome and Gaul. The foundations of the outer walls of most of Wilfrid's church were uncovered when, lately, the new nave of Hexham priory church was begun ; but one of its features has been long known, and is of the highest interest. The crypt for relics below the apse and high altar consists of an oblong chamber, with a western vestibule, approached by a straight stairway from the nave. In addition to the western stair, there are two stairs which communicated with the apse. That on the south side remains perfect, and ends in a passage and vestibule, through which the relic-chamber is entered. The northern stairway leads through a passage to the western vestibule, at the foot of the stair from the nave. The crypt of Wilfrid's contemporary basilica at Ripon also remains: here the arrangement is less complicated; but the arrangement of the main relic-chamber is equally the chief feature of the plan.

§ 15. The foundations of the Saxon church at Peterborough present many difficulties, and may be of a later date than the foundation of the monastery in 655 A.D. But no such difficulties of date or plan exist with regard to the large Saxon church at Brixworth, between Northampton and Market Harborough. Its size and the fact that Roman material has been much re-used in its building, have given rise to the tradition that it is a secular basilica applied to the purposes of a Christian church. As a matter of fact, the Roman brick-work has been re-used in obvious ignorance of Roman methods; so that this circumstance alone would make the legend improbable. The date of the building can hardly be earlier than about 680 A.D., when a monastery was founded here by a colony of monks from Peterborough. The plan originally consisted of (1) a western entrance porch, with a lofty western doorway, and smaller doorways on north and south; (2) a broad nave, divided from the aisles by arches, which spring from large square piers of plain brickwork; (3) a rectangular presbytery, divided from the nave by a screen-wall pierced with three arches; (4) an apsidal chancel, entered from the presbytery by a single arch. On each side of the chancel arch, a doorway entered into a narrow vaulted passage below the ground level, which probably formed an aisle round a crypt below the apse. At a later date, probably in the period of quiet following the later Danish invasions, the apse seems to have been rebuilt, polygonal externally, semi-circular on the inside, and the central crypt-chamber was then possibly filled up. The western porch was also used as the foundation for a tower, and the western arch blocked up with a filling containing a lower doorway, through which the circular turret for the tower-stair was entered. The aisles, either then or at a somewhat later date, having probably fallen into ruin, were removed. The clerestory of the nave remains, with unusually broad round-headed windows.

§ 16. The original plan of Brixworth has points in common with some of the other plans which have been noted. In its triple-arched screen-wall it recalls the Kentish type of church; its rectangular presbytery between nave and apse is a development of the chancel space which existed west of the spring of the apse at St Pancras. It shares its western porch with St Pancras and two, if not four, of the northern group of churches. In the north and south doorways of this porch it has kinship with Monkwearmouth, and at Brixworth there are definite signs that these doorways led into passages which may have been connected with other buildings of the monastery, or possibly even with an *atrium* or fore-court. The aisled nave and the traces of a crypt bring it into relation, not merely with Hexham or Ripon, but with the historical church plan of western Europe generally. At the same time, the plan, regarded as that of an English church, is exceptional. The aisled plan of the parish church was arrived at in spite, not in consequence, of the few early aisled churches which might have supplied it with a model. During the epoch which followed the Danish invasions the aisleless plan was deliberately preferred : the rectangular chancel entirely superseded the apse. No further example of the structural screen-wall occurs. In addition to those mentioned, only three more pre-Conquest examples of crypts are known, and such crypts as occur in parish churches after the Conquest are exceptional, and are usually due to exigencies of site. Only three more aisled churches of unquestion-

ably pre-Conquest date exist above ground. Reculver
has been mentioned. The others are Lydd in Kent,
where only indications of an arcade remain, and the
complete basilican church of Wing, near Leighton
Buzzard, which has a polygonal apse with a crypt
below. Wing is probably much later in date than
most of Brixworth, but one cannot but be struck
by a certain resemblance in construction between the
two naves, and in plan between the crypt at Wing
and the remains of the crypt at Brixworth.

§ 17.   These early churches have been treated at
some length, because they contain certain essential
elements of planning in a state of probation.   The
basilican plan was doubtless the ideal of English
builders during the sixth and early seventh centuries,
but an ideal which was hard to compass where good
building material was not plentiful.   Thus Augustine
and his companions contented themselves in most
instances with a plan which recalled the aisled
basilica, without following out its more elaborate
details.   It is remarkable that they should have
departed from the usual Roman custom, and made
their chancels at the east end of their churches : it is
also remarkable to find at St Pancras the western
porch, the origin of which appears to be the non-
Roman *narthex*.   Models existed, no doubt in the
ruins of the Romano-British churches, which they
repaired ; and we have seen that at Silchester there

is a regular *narthex*, while, on the other hand, there
is a western apse. These models, however, were probably all of one general type, in which the chancel
end was formed by an apsidal projection. When
Roman Christianity reached the north, it had to
contend with the efforts of Celtic missionaries ; and
those efforts were not met by it effectively until, in
664, the energetic leadership of Wilfrid secured a
triumph for his party at the council of Whitby.   Of
the Celtic churches of the north we know but little : it
seems likely that they were for the most part plain
oratories of stone or wood, with or without a separate
chancel. The simplest form, obviously, which a church
can assume is a plain rectangle with an altar at one
end. As the desirability of a special enclosure for
the altar is recognised, a smaller rectangle will be
added at the altar end of the main building, and so
the distinction between nave and chancel will be
formed. There are indications of this natural growth
of plan in some of the early religious buildings in
Ireland.   In remote districts, as in Wales, the simple
nave and chancel plan is general all through the middle
ages; and the smaller country churches often follow
the common Celtic plan of a single rectangle with no
structural division. The ruined chapel at Heysham
in Lancashire, a work of early date, is an undivided
rectangle in plan. This is the form which would
suggest itself naturally to the unskilled builder : the

division of nave and chancel into a larger and smaller rectangle is the next step which would occur to his intelligence in the ordinary course of things. It is possible that Wilfrid and Benedict Biscop found that their aims would be best served by adhering in certain instances to the familiar Celtic plan, and so, while they hired foreign masons and craftsmen to build and furnish their earlier churches, and to set the example of building stone churches after the manner of the Romans, they were careful to avoid the prejudice which insistence on a new plan would have excited. The simplicity, moreover, of a plan like that at Escomb, which requires little architectural skill to work upon, may have been a recommendation ; and the fact that the construction of an apse is more difficult than that of a rectangular chancel must have weighed powerfully with English masons, both at this time and later. The fact remains that, in the early age of our church architecture in stone, the aisled basilica was a rare exception, and the rectangular chancel was, in the north, at least as common as the apse.

CHAPTER II

§ 18. In later Saxon churches the aisleless plan and the rectangular chancel were normal. Instances of an aisled plan after the seventh century have been noted already : it has been seen that there are only two definite examples, and, although there may be indications of others, these are few and far between and uncertain. The apsidal chancel again is exceedingly rare. We have noted it in combination with other basilican features at Wing : the instances in which it occurs again are very few, and in these, as in the important monastic church of Deerhurst, there are other variations from the aisleless plan. In by far the largest number of examples, the plan adhered to was that simple one of which we have a complete prototype at Escomb. Late Saxon fabrics which remain free of later additions are few ; but there is a considerable number of churches which still keep the quoins of an aisleless Saxon nave *in situ,* although aisles have been added during the twelfth

or thirteenth centuries. Such are St Mary-le-Wigford
and St Peter-at-Gowts at Lincoln, Bracebridge in
the western suburb of Lincoln, St Benet's at Cambridge, and Wittering, near Stamford. At Winterton
in Lincolnshire large pieces of the western part of
both walls of the nave were kept as an abutment to
the tower, when aisles were added. Sometimes, as at
Geddington and Brigstock in Northamptonshire, the
whole wall above the nave arcades is the upper part
of the wall of the aisleless building ; and instances in
which blocked window openings, of a not improbably
pre-Conquest date, remain in walls that have subsequently been pierced with arcades, are exceedingly
common. If an untouched Saxon nave is a rare thing,
an unaltered Saxon chancel is obviously rarer. The
small rectangular chancel of the large medieval church
at Repton, in Derbyshire, is practically unique ; it was
probably preserved for the sake of the crypt beneath,
which, at first a plain rectangular chamber, was subsequently, but still in pre-Conquest times, vaulted in
compartments supported by columns. But at Sidbury in Devon, where there is a small rectangular
crypt, the chancel above was rebuilt in the twelfth,
and lengthened in the thirteenth century, without
any reference to the line of the walls of the crypt
below it. A good example of an unaltered late Saxon
fabric is the church of Coln Rogers in Gloucestershire.
Here the western tower, built up inside the nave, is a

later addition, but the nave, rectangular chancel, and arch between them, are still intact. The chancel arch, though by no means broad, is yet much wider than those at Escomb and Bradford-on-Avon; and its width probably represents the normal width of a chancel arch of this period.

§ 19. An addition occurs in most of these late Saxon plans, which had a great influence on the subsequent, and even on the contemporary, development of the church plan. We have noted that at Rome and Ravenna towers formed no part of the original basilican plan, but were added later as *campanili*. In England it appears that the tower formed no part of the plan until, at any rate, the epoch of the Danish wars.

Western bell-towers were very general by the beginning of the eleventh century. In most of these towers, the ground floor forms an entrance porch; but it does not follow that the western tower in England was generated by the heightening of the western porch. The porches of Brixworth and Monk-wearmouth were probably not heightened until the western tower had come into existence elsewhere. An origin for the western tower has been sought in the fore-buildings which occur in some of the early German churches, and contain separate upper chambers. It may be that, derived from this source, the western tower superseded the porch, and, where porches existed, they were adapted to the new fashion.

§ 20. The towers of Earl's Barton, Barnack, and
St Peter's at Barton-on-Humber, are perhaps the most
obviously interesting relics of Saxon architecture
which we possess.   All are much larger in area than
the normal western tower of the later Saxon period.
Earl's Barton is a western tower, and its ground floor
has probably always served as a porch : the rest of
the church, however, is a medieval building of various
periods.   At Barnack, again, the complete plan of the
Saxon church has been lost.   Here, however, the
western tower was something more than a porch.
The doorway is not in the west, but in the south
wall ; and in the west wall, inside the church, is a
niche with a triangular head, which was certainly
neither doorway nor window, but a seat.   Whether
this implies that the ground floor of the tower was
used for special religious functions, or for some purpose connected with the common life of the parish, is
not clear ; but it shows, at any rate, that there was
some good reason for the unusually roomy planning
of the tower.   We stand on firmer ground at Barton-
on-Humber.   Here, again, a large medieval church
exists to the east of the tower.   But upon its western
side is a small rectangular building of contemporary
date, which was not a porch in front of the tower, but
a westward extension of the body of the church, the
main entrances being on either side of the tower. The
foundations of a similar projecting building have

Fig. 4. St Peter's, Barton-on-Humber: from S.W.

been discovered to the east of the tower, beneath
the floor of the later nave. It is therefore clear that
the ground floor of the tower, or rather of a high
tower-like building, formed the body of the church,
and that the eastern projection was the chancel.
There are clear indications at Broughton, also in
north Lincolnshire, that this plan was used, at any
rate, once again. The tower at Broughton is obviously later than that at Barton : the doorway,
whose details are of a post-Conquest character, is in
the south wall ; and a large circular stair-turret, like
that at Brixworth, projects from the west wall.
Probably there was only a chancel here, and no
western annexe to correspond. A similar stair-turret
occurs at Hough-on-the-Hill, between Grantham and
Lincoln : the tower, now western, has a doorway in
the south wall, and probably stands mid-way in date
between Barton and Broughton. It is planned on a
very ample scale, with thin walls and a large floor-
space. The main fabric of the church is altogether
of a later date ; and there are no indications, at any
rate above ground, of an earlier building east of the
tower. The size of the tower, the provision of a
stair-turret, as at Broughton, to leave the ground floor
clear, suggest that here we may have a third example
of the plan in which the tower covered the main body
of the church. The arrangement at Barnack gives
grounds for a suspicion of something of the same kind

there. In all these cases the tower has been a tower from the beginning; but at Barton-on-Humber the uppermost stage was added towards the end of the Saxon period.

§ 21. In these buildings we seem to discover the influence of the centralised plan, acting through the channel of German art. It would be absurd to say that the plan of Barton-on-Humber was inspired by the plan of the palace-church at Aachen, which was an adaptation, with some improvement, of the plan of San Vitale at Ravenna. No masterly intellectual effort, such as the Aachen plan shows, was necessary to plan a rectangle with two smaller rectangles at either end. But the church at Aachen had made the centralised plan familiar to the builders of western Europe. In Germany and in France there are traces of its influence; and we may reasonably suppose that the builders of Barton-on-Humber were acquainted with the existence of an alternative to the usual plan of the church with a longitudinal axis, and did not arrive by haphazard at their concentration of the plan upon a central point. One earlier example of the centralised plan is known to have existed in England. In addition to his basilica at Hexham, Wilfrid had built another church there in the shape of a Greek cross. The description of it which we possess shows that the central space was the actual church, that it was tower-like in form, and

T.	3

nearly circular in shape, and that the arms were
simply porch-like projections. Probably it was a
combination of baptistery with tomb-church. It is
not likely that the simple plan of Barton was derived
from that at Hexham. Both were probably the result
of continental influence; but, while the church at
Hexham may have been the work of Gallo-Roman
masons in direct communication with the general
current of architectural progress, the church at Barton was probably built by Englishmen, who adapted
the centralised plan to methods natural to their com-
parative want of skill.

§ 22. Neither at this time nor later did the
centralised plan in England develop along the lines
suggested by Barton-on-Humber. No real development on such lines was possible. In Germany, the
achievement at Aachen made possible the polygonal
nave of St Gereon at Cologne and the centralised
plan of the Liebfrauenkirche at Trier, as well as
many twelfth and thirteenth century churches whose
complicated parts are planned and massed together
with relation to a central tower space. In England,
however, the habit of dealing with circular or polygonal forms made little progress; and our few "round
churches," the plan of the naves of which was a
devout imitation of the church of the Holy Sepulchre
at Jerusalem, and our polygonal chapter houses, are
almost all that we have to show in the way of attempts

at a definitely centralised plan. Our church plan
develops as the result of an effort to combine a series
of rectangles effectively; and, while this combination
can be attempted in several different ways, it is
obvious that the rigid lines of the rectangle do not
admit of that free scope in centralised planning which
is given by the circle or polygon.

§ 23. We have seen, however, that, even in the
earliest days, there was a tendency to admit additions
to the simple longitudinal plan, which, in process of
time, were bound to give birth, if not to a definitely
centralised plan, to something, at any rate, in which
a central point counted for much. A feature of the
early cathedral and of St Pancras at Canterbury, was
the projection of *porticus*, porches or side chapels,
from the nave. These were entered by archways
pierced in the centre of the lateral walls. In the
cathedral they had outer doorways, and formed the
main entrances of the church, on the north from the
monastery, on the south from the city. The south
porch contained the altar of St Gregory, and, as
Eadmer tells us, was used as a court of justice to
which litigants, in process of time, resorted from
every part of England. In the north porch, dedicated
to St Martin, was held the school of the monastery.
Upon both porches towers were built at a date which
cannot be ascertained, but was probably later than
the time of Augustine. Of the use of the porches at

St Pancras, which did not contain outer doorways, it
is impossible to say anything definitely. Entrance
porches, of which one remains, projected from the
sides of the church at Bradford-on-Avon: the
outer and inner doorways of the north porch are
extremely narrow, and are placed west of the centre
of its north and south walls. It is possible, therefore, that there was an altar in this porch, so that it
served the double purpose of entrance porch and side
chapel.

§ 24.   As time went on, the western porch beneath
the tower was disused as a public entrance. The
principal entrance of most churches is on the south
side, west of the centre of the aisle wall, and is
usually covered by a porch. There is a Saxon ex-
example of this at Bishopstone in Sussex, where, as
at Bradford, room seems to have been left for an
altar on the east side. However, the main entrance
of the ordinary Saxon church was at the west end,
through the ground floor of the tower. The porch in
the lateral wall seems to have been regarded primarily
as a side chapel ; and in some later Saxon churches
the porches were dissociated from lateral doorways,
and were planned as closed projections from the
eastern part of the north and south walls of the
nave. This seems to have happened at Britford,
near Salisbury, where archways remain on both sides
near the east end of the nave. At Deerhurst square

projections were entered from both sides of the nave, immediately west of the chancel arch; and it is probable that there were somewhat similar projections at Repton. At Worth in Sussex, where the north and south doorways of the nave are Saxon, and there is no western entrance or original tower, there are large Saxon chapels projecting from the eastern part of the nave, and entered by wide arches. The cruciform plan is sufficiently marked in the conjectural restorations of Deerhurst and Repton. At Worth it is quite unmistakable.

§ 25. At Worth, however, in spite of the dignity of the lateral arches, the chapels are still porch-like excrescences, larger in scale than usual, but lower in elevation than the nave. In elevation their transept-like appearance is less noticeable than on plan. Moreover, the length of the nave remains unbroken from west wall to chancel arch : no central space is marked off to which these transeptal projections give emphasis. Nevertheless, a suggestion of an intermediate space between nave and chancel is given ; and this space is definitely marked in the plans of churches which may be quite as early in date as Worth—*i.e.* about the first half of the eleventh century—by the admission of a tower between nave and chancel. The eastern part of the walls of the nave at St Mary's in Dover Castle are continued upwards as a tower, with small rectangular chapels projecting

from the sides of the ground floor. Externally, no
division between the tower and nave is noticeable ;
but, inside the church, in addition to the chancel arch
and the arches into the chapels, a fourth arch is pierced
in the western wall of the tower, and so an intermediate space between tower and nave is effectually
created. At Breamore in Hants, a further step is
taken. The tower space, between nave and chancel,
is of the same width as the nave ; but, in addition to
the necessary internal division, an external division
is also marked by the quoins of the tower, which are
complete to the ground. Only one chapel remains
at Breamore, on the south of the tower, entered by
a narrow Saxon archway ; but there was originally
another on the north.

§ 26. The chapels which project from these early
" central " towers are, it is to be noted, not true transepts. They are narrower than the tower, which is
built up from the ground, and not upon a system
of piers and arches which require lateral abutments
in the form of transepts. The western tower is
transferred, as it were, to a point near the centre
of the church, assumes the width of the nave, and is
provided with transeptal excrescences, to communicate with which its side walls are pierced. Such
excrescences are not necessary. At Stanton Lacy,
in Shropshire, there is only one. At Dunham Magna,
in Norfolk, and other places, such as Waith in

Lincolnshire, there are, or were originally, none at all. The construction of the "central" tower upon piers connected by arches was beyond the skill of the ordinary Saxon builder; and its natural consequence, the development of the full cruciform plan, with transepts of the height and width of nave and chancel, was thus out of his reach. We know, from contemporary evidence, that one important abbey church, that of Ramsey, had a central tower which was built upon piers and arches as early as 974 A.D.; and perhaps this was the case in other large churches. But, even in the large church of Stow in Lincolnshire, which is commonly taken on trust, without sufficient historical evidence, as the cathedral church of the Saxon diocese of Lindsey, although an advance in transeptal construction was made, the main principle was imperfectly grasped. This church was made the home of a community of clergy about the beginning of the reign of Edward the Confessor, by Leofric, earl of Mercia, and his wife Godiva. It was restored after the Conquest by Rémi, the first Norman bishop of Lincoln. The aisleless nave and chancel are Norman work of two periods: probably the nave was rebuilt upon Saxon foundations. The transepts, however, of considerable length and equal height with nave and chancel, were retained from the pre-Conquest building. The tall jambs of the arches of the central tower also remain on all four sides.

The arches which they bear are of early Norman
character; and the present tower is a late Gothic
structure, the arches and piers of which are built
up on the inner side of the older masonry.   But the
Saxon tower space, including the area of the arch-
jambs, is rather wider than the arms of the cross
which project from it.   The tower formed a separate
building, with quoins complete from the ground, and
nave, chancel, and transepts, instead of combining to
support it, were mere excrescences from it, entered
by arches in its walls.   Possibly the example of
Barton-on-Humber may have had to do with this
treatment of the tower as a separate central pavi-
lion, which may have been deliberately preferred to
the arch and pier treatment.   In other respects the
plan is an advance upon the plans of Dover and
Breamore.   And the necessary advance upon Stow
is found in the church of Norton-on-Tees in south
Durham.   Here the tower, between nave and chancel,
rests on piers connected by arches.   The arches have
been widened; two have been entirely rebuilt at
a later date; and the rest of the church has been
subjected at different times to enlargement and rebuilding.   In spite of this, we have at Norton our
earliest surviving example of a plan in which the
various portions of the church—nave, chancel, and
transepts—are gathered together in one structural
connexion.   The tower is to the east of the centre of

the longitudinal axis of the church; but structurally, it is the central point with regard to which the building is planned, and the unity of the composition depends upon it.

§ 27. We have arrived thus at a centralised plan of cruciform shape, of which the component parts are rectangular, the central space being approximately a square. The examples which have been given cannot be proved to follow one another in chronological order, but they represent successive steps in planning and construction, of which Norton-on-Tees is the highest. The importance of the inclusion of the tower in the plan is obvious. In its early appearances, its position is unsettled, but the natural tendency is to place it above a main entrance ; and this is usually at the west end of the building. Where the builders aim at a simple centralised plan, the high central rectangle will form, like the round or octagonal central space of Wilfrid's church of St Mary at Hexham, *ecclesia...in modum turris erecta*, and, as at Barton-on-Humber, will possibly be heightened by a later generation into a real tower. The distinction of the side chapel from the entrance porches, becoming more fully recognised, will lead to the building of transeptal chapels at the east end of the nave; and thus an important addition will be made to the ordinary longitudinal plan. The need of some central building, against which these

additions may abut, will be felt. The tower will
thus be introduced between nave and chancel, either
as an independent structure, or as an upward extension of part of the side walls. The transepts
thus, as at Stow, can be raised to an equal height
with nave and chancel. From this to a plan in
which the component parts are recognised as inter-
dependent, and are closely knit together in structural
unity, is an obvious step. At this point, architectural
skill, as distinct from mere building ingenuity, comes
into play.

§ 28. As we proceed, we shall find survivals of
old plans, even at an advanced period in the middle
ages, which prove that progress in architecture was
by no means of an uniform kind. Builders in remote,
and especially in hilly, districts, from Saxon times to
the present day, have naturally restricted themselves
to plans which require as little cost as possible to
carry out. Local building material is also an important consideration. In districts where good building
stone is to be obtained on the spot, or where money
is plentiful and water carriage is possible, the development of plan is naturally rapid, and every fifty
years or so, additions to churches will be made in
which the old plan will become entirely transformed.
In woodland districts, the plan will be controlled to
no small extent by the requirements of timber construction. In such regions, Saxon churches were

probably built of wood. The only wooden church of Saxon times which remains is that of Greenstead in south Essex, with a rectangular chancel and aisleless nave constructed of vertical logs placed side by side, and framed originally into a timber plinth. However, it may be stated as a general rule, that, whatever may be the helps or hindrances to development provided by local materials, the real starting-point of the parish church plan of the middle ages is in every part of the country an aisleless plan ; and that this plan consists either of a nave and chancel with a longitudinal axis, or of a nave and chancel whose longitudinal axis is intersected by a transverse axis across transepts. Variations, no doubt, occur ; but these will never carry us far from one or other of these fundamental plans. The aisled basilica of the continent found no scope for itself in Saxon England ; and it was through an interval of aisleless building that the aisled plan eventually became acclimatised, and then in a form which bears only a superficial kinship to the basilican plan.

CHAPTER III

§ 29. During the century after the Norman
Conquest, the great abbey churches and cathedrals
represent the work of a foreign architectural school,
gradually acclimatising itself in England; while, on
the other hand, the parish church continued to be
planned by local men, open to receive the improvements which more skilled foreign masons had introduced. Consequently, while local art received a
continually increasing refinement, the plan of the
church developed upon traditional lines, and not upon
those novel lines which foreign masons would have
laid down for it. The chief proof of this is seen in
the persistence of the aisleless plan with rectangular
chancel and western tower. The tendency of a
Norman builder would be to design his church with
an apsidal chancel, transepts, and a central tower:
his practice would vary, but this would be his
favourite plan. On the other hand, the rectangular
chancel and western tower remained the favourite
terminations of the parish church in England. But,

while a large number of rubble-built, unbuttressed Norman towers, usually heightened or otherwise altered in the later middle ages, remain in many parts of England, their relation to the plan suffers some change. The ground floor of the Saxon tower was, as we have noticed, the main entrance to the church. The Norman western tower either contained no western doorway at all, or provided merely an

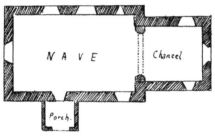

Fig. 5. Aisleless plan : 12th century.

entrance, which was used only on special occasions. At Caistor the ground floor was probably the main porch of the aisleless church ; and there are exceptional instances, as at Finchingfield in Essex, where, in fairly advanced Norman work, the same arrangement was clearly contemplated. On the other hand, at Laceby, between Caistor and Grimsby, a south doorway, coeval with the western tower, has always been the main entrance to the church.

Similarly, at Hooton Pagnell, and at Blatherwycke in Northamptonshire, south doorways, of the same age as the tower, form the chief entrance. These last three are early Norman examples; but we may go back even further, to find the same thing in churches which are usually reckoned as late Saxon work, at Heapham in Lincolnshire, and Kirk Hammerton, between York and Boroughbridge. In south Yorkshire there are a few churches of the middle of the twelfth century whose western towers are noticeably derived, in their plan and general construction, from the Saxon type—Birkin, Brayton, and Riccall. But in all three, the main entrance to the church was made through a south doorway, the arch of which is covered with elaborate late Norman ornaments. The western tower was thus reduced to the state of a bell-tower at one end of the church, and, while increasing in size and in magnificence, was actually a less indispensable part of the plan than before.

§ 30. The nave of the Norman aisleless church was usually short, and, where the church was entirely rebuilt, rather wide in proportion to its length. The naves of churches like Garton-on-the-Wolds or Kirkburn in Yorkshire, give the effect of spacious halls, of no great length, but wide and lofty. It cannot be doubted, however, that the fabric of the Saxon church was frequently kept, or that the church was rebuilt upon Saxon foundations. It is not unusual, as already stated, to find Saxon quoins still existing at the angles of naves to which aisles have subsequently been added. Evidences, on the other hand, of the westward lengthening of a Saxon nave in the Norman period appear to be rare. At North Witham in south Lincolnshire, the south and (blocked) north doorways are Norman work, in the usual position near the west end of the nave. East of them, however, in the centre of the nave walls, there are distinct traces of the inner openings of a north and south doorway, which may belong to the late Saxon period. That we have here a case of the twelfth century lengthening of an earlier nave may be inferred. The probability is increased by the fact that, in the neighbouring church of Colsterworth, where aisles were added during the early Norman period to a late Saxon fabric, the nave and aisles, towards the end of the twelfth century, were certainly extended a bay westward. As little architectural work is done without a precedent, we may assume that the builders at Colsterworth were following the example of North Witham.

§ 31. The great majority of Norman rectangular chancels have been lengthened and enlarged ; for the plain "altar-house" at the east end of the nave was too small for the purposes of the ritual of the thirteenth and fourteenth centuries, and afforded no intermediate space between nave and chancel. However, short and approximately square chancels were by no means invariable ; and, before the middle of the twelfth century, oblong chancels of considerable length in proportion to their width were being built. There is a good early twelfth century example at Moor Monkton, in the Ainsty of York ; and the chancel of the middle of the twelfth century at Earl's Barton, Northants, is of considerable depth, and was of ample size for all later purposes. At Earl's Barton the eastern portion was the chancel proper ; while the western portion supplied that space for a quire which was not provided in less elongated plans. In by far the larger number of cases, the rectangular chancel had a wooden roof. There is, however, a fair number of churches in which the system of ribbed vaulting, as employed in larger buildings, was used. Thus at Heddon-on-the-Wall, Northumberland, there is a small square chancel with a ribbed vault. At Warkworth, there is a long vaulted chancel of two bays, built during the first quarter of the twelfth century ; and at Tickencote, Rutland, two bays are combined in one by the use of sexpartite vaulting. In these cases the chancel arches are wide, forming the western transverse arches of the vaulting : that at Tickencote is of remarkable magnificence.

§ 32. There are certain cases in which the chancel was of the same width as the nave, and no structural division existed between them. At Askham Bryan and at the chapel of Copmanthorpe, near York, the plan, externally and internally, is a plain undivided oblong. At Tansor, Northants, the chancel was rebuilt about 1140, when the side walls were set back in a line with those of the nave. In St Mary's in the Castle at Leicester, the long and very narrow nave was, as may still be clearly seen, continued eastward without a break into the long and narrow quire and chancel. Here the eastern half was used, no doubt, by the college of dean and canons, while the western half was the parish church. The beautiful church of St Peter, Northampton, built towards the end of the third quarter of the twelfth century, gives us a complete example of an undivided plan, aisled throughout save in the eastern bay, which forms a projecting chancel east of the aisles of the choir.

§ 33. Hitherto we have dealt merely with the rectangular chancel. But there are also churches which end in an eastern apse. These are comparatively few and exceptional. In Yorkshire, where the number of Norman rectangular chancels is large, and buildings such as Adel exhibit the aisleless church in its highest state of architectural development, the number of apsidal chancels can be counted on the fingers of one hand. In Sussex, where Caen stone was largely used, and we should expect foreign influence to be noticeable, the proportion of apsidal chancels is small. In Gloucestershire, the Cotswold district contains several small Norman churches, which have been little altered : the rectangular chancel is universal. These are typical districts ; and, to state a general rule, we may say that, while the apsidal chancel is foreign to no part of England, and occurs in unexpected places, as in the chapel of Old Bewick, Northumberland, it is never general in any single region. Its rarity is an important fact. Were our parish churches the work of masons sent out from the larger churches and monasteries, we should expect to find it a common feature ; for in those buildings the apsidal plan prevailed. But, in the hands of local masons, its sparing employment is easily explained. To build an apse needs skill, not only in planning, but in stone-cutting. The question of vaulting the apse increases the difficulty and the expense. These difficulties would not trouble masons who had worked at the building of Durham or Ely or Winchester ; nor would expense trouble the monasteries, which, according to the popular idea, were so ready to lavish money on the fabrics of parish churches. Many apsidal chancels have disappeared, no doubt ; but, if we take the bulk of

Fig. 6. Birkin, Yorkshire: interior.

those which remain into account, we shall find that they have a habit of occurring in small groups, as in Berkshire, where three occur together within a single old rural deanery, and that the large majority of the churches in which they are found were not monastic property. A few belonged to preceptories of Knights Templars in their neighbourhood ; and perhaps we may see in their apses a reference to the circular form of the Holy Sepulchre. But, as a rule, we may say that a band of masons in certain neighbourhoods developed some skill in building apses, that money was forthcoming, and that so a few examples came into existence. In one curious instance, Langford in Essex, which is within easy distance of four or five other apsed churches, there is an apse at the west, and there are foundations of another at the east end of the building. For this church a Saxon origin has been claimed : the plan, at any rate, indicates a survival of a plan once common in western Christendom, and especially in the German provinces. In apsed churches, like Birkin in Yorkshire, the apse does not spring from points directly east of the chancel arch. The arch is wide and lofty ; behind it is a nearly square rectangular space, which is divided from the apse by another arch. At Birkin the apse has ribbed vaulting, which allows the walls to be pierced freely for windows. At Copford in Essex, Old Bewick, and other places, the roof is a half-dome without ribs : this allows for the display of mural painting, but admits of less light.

§ 34. The most important feature in the apsidal plan is the provision of the distinctly marked quire space between the nave and chancel. This space also occurs in plans where the chancel is rectangular; but in such cases it becomes the ground story of a tower. There are famous examples of this at Iffley, near Oxford, and Studland in Dorset, where the chancels are vaulted. Coln St Denis in Gloucestershire, where the tower is of very wide area, and projects noticeably north and south of nave and chancel; and Christon in Somerset, are further instances of the plan. The tower between nave and chancel, without transepts, is seldom found in an apsidal plan. It occurs at Newhaven in Sussex, where there is a small apse. Here the plan is virtually that of some small parish churches in Normandy, such as Yainville, near Jumièges. The majority of such plans in England, however, end in a rectangular chancel. Precedent for the plan is, as we have seen, to be found in Saxon churches. At St Pancras, Canterbury, we have noticed the westward prolongation of the apse : at Brixworth a definite presbytery or quire space was planned, on a large scale, between apse and nave. In later Saxon churches, where the chancel was rectangular,

a tower, with or without transeptal chapels, was
sometimes built between nave and chancel; and
here, although externally the division was not
always clearly marked, an internal quire space
was divided off from the nave by the western arch
of the tower. The aisleless plan, therefore, with
a tower above the quire, and a rectangular chancel,
points to a development along old-fashioned lines,
even in churches in which, as at Iffley, the builders
have acquired great skill in expressing themselves in
Norman terms. In certain districts, as in Gloucestershire, this plan was a favourite one. Even in the
fourteenth century, Leckhampton church, near
Cheltenham, was rebuilt in faithful adherence to
this tradition. Here the tower is narrower than
the small chancel, and the nave has a south aisle.

§ 35. In the cases of Dover, Breamore, Stow,
and Norton, we have watched the gradual evolution
of the cruciform plan with central tower. It must
be noted once more that to the cruciform plan the
central tower built on piers and arches is essential.
It is possible, as in the Gloucestershire churches
of Almondsbury and Avening, to pierce the north
and south walls of a tower and add transeptal
chapels: the plan will have a cruciform appearance,
but will still be only an elongated plan with lateral
additions. It is possible, in a church where there
is no central tower at all, to extend the side

walls at right angles north and south, and so form transepts; but here again the transepts have no structural reference to a central point in the plan, but are mere widenings of the nave or

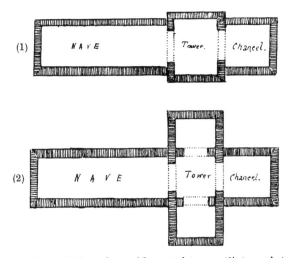

Fig. 7. Two aisleless plans with central tower: (1) tower between nave and chancel; (2) tower over crossing of transepts with nave and chancel.

aisles. The thirteenth century aisleless churches of Potterne, in Wiltshire, and Acton Burnell, in Shropshire, are both cruciform in plan. The church at Potterne was planned throughout with reference to

the crossing of transepts, nave, and quire, above
which its central tower rose : the tower space is the
central point of the whole. But, at Acton Burnell,
there is no central tower or space : the body of the
church consists of a long aisleless nave and an
aisleless chancel beyond ; and the transeptal chapels
are simply stuck on, as it were, to the eastern part
of either wall of the nave. This is at once noticeable
in elevation, when the chapels are seen to be mere
excrescences, with roofs lower than the nave. Moreover, where there is a true central crossing, with
a tower above, such as we find in almost all our
cathedrals, a transept on either side is necessary
for the support of the tower. The transepts need
not be wholly symmetrical, although in most cases
they are ; but they must be there. On the other
hand, where there is no central tower, and the
crossing is merely apparent, symmetry of treatment
is quite unnecessary. While there are two transeptal
chapels of similar size at Acton Burnell, or at
Achurch in Northamptonshire, there are far more
instances in which a less regular treatment was
adopted. Thus, at Childs Wickham in Gloucestershire, and Montacute in Somerset, there is only
one transeptal chapel, in each case on the north
side. At Corbridge in Northumberland, transeptal
chapels, extended outwards from the aisle walls,
are of different lengths. At Medbourne in Leicester-

Fig. 8. North Newbald, Yorkshire : tower arches, chancel
and S. transept, from N.W.

shire, a long aisleless transeptal chapel was built
out from the north side of the nave in the thirteenth
century. Within the next fifty years a south chapel
was built, but, instead of copying the proportions
of the northern chapel symmetrically, the builders
gave their new chapel a much greater width, and
placed its altars in an eastern aisle. The plan is
thus accidentally cruciform. At Acton Burnell and
Achurch it is, no doubt, designedly cruciform; at
Montacute and Childs Wickham, imperfectly cruciform. But all three varieties belong to one class,
the longitudinal plan with transeptal extensions.
The structural feature which makes the truly cruciform plan, the central tower upon arches and piers,
is wanting. And this distinction between churches
planned from a centre, and churches whose plan
follows a longitudinal axis, although often overlooked, is essential.

§ 36. A noble example of a Norman cruciform
church, whose plan has suffered little alteration,
exists at North Newbald in the east Riding of
Yorkshire. At each angle of the crossing are
masses of shafted piers, connected by wide and
lofty rounded arches. The nave, as is usual, is the
longest arm of the four, so that the plan is a Latin
cross. It has north and south doorways: there are
also doorways in the end walls of the transepts,
placed in the western part of each wall. In the

east wall of each transept is an arch, now blocked
up, the filling being pierced with fifteenth century
windows. These arches are the openings of original
apses, which contained the transept altars. The
chancel, probably always rectangular, was rebuilt
in the fifteenth century. As a corollary of the true
cruciform plan, the four arms are all of equal width.
At Bampton-in-the-Bush, Oxon, where the plan of
the church was greatly altered in the thirteenth
century by the addition of aisles, the Norman plan
was very similar to that of North Newbald. The
cruciform plan of Melbourne, Derbyshire, with its
aisled nave, was probably inspired more directly by
continental examples. The aisleless chancel was
vaulted, and ended in an apse, which was squared
in later times by the addition of a rectangular piece
east of its springing points. Out of the east walls
of the short transepts opened wide apses, the walls
of which joined the western ends of the walls of the
chancel. Thus, externally, the plan of the eastern
part of the church was closely allied to the plan with
three apses which, in some of our larger churches,
was derived from Normandy. At Melbourne, however,
there are important variations from this plan. The
chancel is short, there are no quire aisles, and the
transept apses were rounded externally. In the larger
churches of Normandy, the side apses were at the
end of the quire aisles, and were usually squared

externally, while the apses projecting from the east walls of the transepts, as at Saint-Georges-de-Boscherville, were left rounded. At Newbald and Bampton there seems to have been no attempt to give complete unity of design, as at Melbourne, to the rectangular chancel and transeptal apses. In any case, transeptal apses were the exception in the plans of our Norman cruciform churches, although their convenience for holding altars is obvious.

§ 37. The cruciform plan, beautiful as it is, was never generally adopted. It was inconvenient for purposes of public worship, as long as the rounded arch remained fashionable. In our own day, even in churches where the central tower is carried on high pointed arches, and the view of the altar is practically unhindered, the chancel is cut off from the nave by the crossing, and the acoustic problem, which in modern church planning is so necessary a consideration, is almost insurmountable. In the middle ages, this problem was not so acute ; but it was undesirable that the interior of the chancel should be nearly invisible from the nave. At Newbald the tower arches are planned upon a liberal scale: at Bampton, on the other hand, where the eastern tower arch is left, the others having been rebuilt in the thirteenth century, it is very low. The low tower arches at Burford, Oxon, and the narrow arches at St Giles,

Northampton, are examples of the way in which the supports of the Norman central tower interfered with the internal convenience of churches. It was not until much later that this difficulty was solved, and then only in one or two cases, when the cruciform plan had become exceptional. The plans of Bampton, Burford, and Witney, show how the builders of west Oxfordshire experimented in cruciform planning. The division between chancel and nave is felt much less at Witney than in the other two churches ; for the great thirteenth century tower and spire, resting upon massive piers joined by pointed arches, throw a considerable portion of their weight upon nave and transept arcades, whose exceptional massiveness gives unity to the whole design. In the fifteenth century, however, the rebuilders of the aisleless church of Minster Lovell, between Witney and Burford, solved the problem by removing the supports of their square central tower from the angles of the crossing to points entirely within the church, and building arches from the piers thus formed to the angles of the crossing. The comparatively light piers, instead of hindering the view, allow of easy access from the nave to the transepts, and there is hardly a point in the body of the church from which seeing and hearing alike are in any way impeded. With the earlier builders, however, the natural course was to leave the piers where they were, and endeavour to lighten them as far as possible; and, in aisled churches, the difficulties involved often led to the abandonment of the complete cruciform plan.

§ 38. The cruciform church gives occasion for a brief remark on one aspect of medieval building which is often exaggerated. The revival of interest in medieval architecture, in the early part of the nineteenth century, was accompanied by an insistence on symbolism in the plan and design of churches. A minute symbolism, which often was the fruit of pious imagination, or was derived from the fancies of post-medieval writers on ritual, was read into every detail of the medieval church fabric. It is true that, as has been said, some builders worked imaginatively, imitating in the round naves of a few churches the rotunda of the Holy Sepulchre. Other instances of devout imitation might be found, if we looked for them. But the imitation of a concrete model is a different thing from translating abstract mysteries into the plan and elevation of a building. And, although the ground plan with nave, transepts, and chancel, certainly forms a cross ; and, although, as time went on, the resemblance to the chief symbol of the Christian faith was no doubt recognised and valued, the plan itself, as we have shown, came into being from entirely natural causes. Where the central tower was introduced, the plan was dictated by structural necessity. Where there was no central tower, transeptal chapels provided accommodation for altars, for which the body of the church afforded no convenience. In this and in other cases, medieval builders were impelled by practical common sense and the requirements of the services of the church; and symbolism, if it was a consideration at all, was purely secondary.

CHAPTER IV

§ 39. The variations of the aisleless plan, which
have been indicated, are all of which it is capable.
Naturally, after the twelfth century, many aisleless
churches were still built, and are common in country
districts. In their humblest form we find them in
the small churches of highland regions, the masonry
of which is so rough that their date is often a matter
of doubt. Sometimes they have been rebuilt, with
a lengthened chancel, as at West Heslerton, near
Scarborough. In many instances, we have aisleless
country churches rebuilt in the fourteenth and fifteenth centuries, with western towers. This, uncommon in no part of England, is especially common in
Norfolk and Suffolk ; and some of these churches,
like Ranworth in Norfolk, have much dignity and
spaciousness of proportion. In some late Gothic
churches the structural division between nave and
chancel is left out, and the building has been deliberately planned as a spacious aisleless rectangle,

of which the eastern bay is allotted to the chancel.
This happens at Temple Balsall in Warwickshire
and the chapel of South Skirlaugh in Yorkshire.
Aisleless plans with one or two transeptal chapels
are to be found all through the middle ages : Acton
Burnell represents a thoroughly symmetrical employment of this type. On the other hand, aisleless
cruciform plans with central towers are by no means
common after the twelfth century. Potterne is a
perfect development of this plan in the thirteenth
century. There is a complete aisleless cruciform
plan at Othery, near Bridgwater, where the tall
central tower is quite out of proportion to the
humble church above which it rises, and has necessi-
tated substantial outer buttressing. Here probably
the church was rebuilt on earlier foundations, transepts being possibly added. In many instances an
aisleless cruciform church seems to have been rebuilt
on the lines of a complete Norman plan. This was
with little doubt the case at Acaster Malbis, near
York, where the church is planned with direct relation
to the central space, but without a tower ; and the
foundations of earlier walls can be traced all round
the building, at the foot of the walls built in the
fourteenth century. The absence of the tower is an
anomaly, but is one method of solving the problem
of the connexion between nave and chancel in the
cruciform plan.

§ 40. Thus, if here and there we can detect novelties which make for improvements upon the aisleless plan, the plan itself is subject to no general development upon its own unelastic lines. The real course of development is to be traced in the gradual addition of aisles to the church. Just as the basilica may have come into existence by the addition of aisles to an aisleless building, so the parish church was enlarged by the piercing of its walls for columns and arches, and the incorporation of aisles with the main building. The usefulness of aisles is at once apparent. They afford greater space for the distribution of the congregation. The aisleless church may be inconveniently crowded from wall to wall : on the other hand, where spaces are left between the nave and side walls, the congregation will mass itself in the nave, but the aisles will be left free until the nave is filled, and thus there will be free access through the side doorways for as long a time as possible. Aisles also afford a clear space for processions, and allow them to turn inside the church at a certain point and without difficulty. In addition to this, aisles form a convenient situation for the smaller altars of a church, and, from an early date, were added with this view.

§ 41. A parish church usually contained more than one altar, even if served by a single priest. In the small aisleless church of Patricio in Brecon-

shire, in addition to the altar in the chancel, there
were two smaller altars, which still remain in place,
on either side of the central doorway of the rood
screen. Such altars were dedicated in honour of
various saints ; and mass would be said at them on
the festivals of those saints and on other occasions.
The various popular devotions which came into being
in the middle ages, led to the multiplication of special
altars and chapels. In cathedral and abbey churches,
where there were many priests, the provision of
a number of altars was, from the first, a necessity.
To this is due the adoption, from the beginning, of the
aisled plan in our larger churches, where it is a direct
inheritance from the basilican plan. At Norwich
and at Gloucester, for instance, the apse was provided
with an encircling aisle, which gave access to small
apsidal chapels. The transepts also had eastern
chapels ending in apses. At Durham each transept
had an eastern aisle, containing a row of such
chapels ; and the abnormal development of the
transepts in thirteenth century churches, as at
York, Lincoln, and Salisbury, and the occasional
provision of an eastern transept, or of a great transverse eastern arm, like the Nine Altars at Fountains
and Durham, was made with a view to the continually
growing number of altars and daily masses. In
Cistercian abbeys, the churches of which were
wholly devoted to the uses of the monastery,

the aisles of the nave were divided into chapels
by transverse walls. In the secular cathedral of
Chichester, where the aisles had to be left free,
outer aisles, similarly divided, were made. Great
French cathedrals, like Amiens, not only have a
complicated series of chapels opening from the
aisles of the apse, but have their naves lined
with chapels, which were formed by removing the
outer walls of the aisles to a level with the outer
face of the buttresses. The ordinary parish church
had no need of these elaborate arrangements, although in towns and in districts where money was
plentiful and its possessors recognised its true source,
plans hardly less spacious than those of the cathedral
and monastery churches came into being. But it is
obvious that, in a church where there were no more
than two or three altars, space would be gained by
removing them from the body of the church to the
end of the aisles. In some twelfth century churches
there were probably altars against the wall on either
side of the narrow chancel arch ; and, in later days,
as at Ranworth and Patricio, when the rood screen
filled the lower part of a broad arch, altars were
placed against the screen. In the first case, the
chancel arch might have been widened ; in the second
case, the sides of the screen would have been freed,
by the addition of aisles into which the altars could
have been removed.

§ 42. The most common plan of the aisled church is formed by an aisled nave with a long aisleless chancel, western tower, and south porch. So common is this that it may be spoken of as the normal plan of the larger English parish church. There must have been, we already have said, a very large number of aisleless churches in England at the time of the Conquest. Where Norman builders reconstructed parish churches, they showed a distinct preference for the aisleless plan. But, in many churches, built about or soon after the beginning of the twelfth century, aisles were planned and executed. The walls of earlier churches were entirely taken down, and new arcades built in their place, not necessarily on the precise line of the old foundations. Aisled twelfth century naves on a magnificent scale may be seen, for example, at Melbourne in Derbyshire, and Sherburn-in-Elmet, between York and Leeds. Both places were important episcopal residences : Melbourne belonged to the bishops of Carlisle ; the manor of Sherburn was the head of a barony of the archbishops of York, who, all through the middle ages, did much to promote architecture on their domains. Another twelfth century nave of great magnificence is that of Norham-on-Tweed, which belonged to the cathedral priory of Durham ; and, although we must not assume that it was built at the expense of the monastery, it doubtless owes its stately

proportions to the influence of the mother house.
Less imposing in elevation, but richer in refined
detail, are such aisled naves as those of Long Sutton
in south Lincolnshire, and Walsoken in west Norfolk,
which belong to the later part of the twelfth century.
The plans in each case are very regular ; and the
new arcades were probably built, at any rate in
part, on older foundations. These naves reach the
extent, unusual in a parish church, of seven bays.
The nave of Norham is of five bays. Melbourne
has five bays, but the plan of the church was as
exceptional at the west as at the east end. Western
towers were planned, but not completed, at the end
of either aisle : this feature, probably imitated
from Southwell minster, was also contemplated at
Bakewell in Derbyshire. Between the towers was
an extra western bay of the nave, divided into
two stories, the lower forming a vaulted return
aisle, the upper forming a gallery. There are
only four bays at Sherburn, but here the aisles
were continued as far as the western face of the
tower. The tower is thus engaged within the aisles,
and its vaulted ground floor forms, like the western
bay at Melbourne, a return to them.

§ 43. But, when the question of adding aisles to
a church arose, the builders were met by the difficulty
that the church was wanted constantly for service.
The taking down of the walls and the building of new

arcades interfered with this necessary use of the
fabric. In our own day a congregation, driven out
by builders or restorers, can resort to a school room
or mission room. In the middle ages, these alter-
natives were unknown; and the church was positively
indispensable. With this in view, the builders were
obliged to add their aisles without touching more of
the main fabric than they could help. Usually, then,
they took the length of the existing aisleless building
for the length of their aisles. They then set out the
aisles upon either side of the church, building the
outer walls, and dividing them into bays by external
buttresses. Then, opposite each buttress, they proceeded to break through the walls of the church.
Leaving a piece of the old wall to serve as a
footing for each column, they built up the columns
in the thickness of the wall, the masonry being
gradually removed as each rose in height. The
arches were made in the same way, the wall being
removed by degrees until the two sides of each arch
met at the key-stone. The aisles were then roofed,
and, finally, the masses of wall which still remained
beneath each arch were broken down, and the nave
and aisles thrown into one. The old masonry could
be removed through the doorways of the aisles; and
sometimes one of the end walls of either aisle was
left unbuilt to the last, so that the masons could
have free entrance for new, and exit for old, material.

The old walls of the nave, above the columns and arches, were left untouched. In this way the upper parts of the walls of several Saxon naves—more,

Fig. 9.   Gretton, Northants: arcade of nave showing blocked window head.

probably, than we have opportunity of discovering —remain to us. The north wall at Geddington in Northamptonshire is the most striking instance.

The practice was so common as to be general. In
hundreds of country churches the plinths on which
the columns of the nave rest are probably pieces of
the foundation of the older wall, refaced, or even left in
the rough. Instances are nearly as common in which
the heads of the new arches have blocked earlier
windows ; for, in the eleventh and twelfth centuries,
when glass was rare and expensive, and the openings
were usually closed by latticed shutters, the windows
were set high in the wall. There is a remarkable
example of the retention of old work at Seamer, near
Scarborough. To this fine twelfth century aisleless
church a north aisle was added in the fifteenth
century. The builders, possibly wishing to avoid
expense, employed the old method, which in those
days of prosperity and general rebuilding had fallen
into disuse. In order not to interfere with the older
windows, they deliberately made their arches very
low : the result is that, from the interior of the aisle,
one can see that the old wall was almost entirely
kept, the new columns being built up on the line of
the flat pilaster buttresses, which were left unaltered
above the capitals. Sometimes, the connexion between
nave and aisles was made by cutting arches at intervals in the wall, without building columns. The
north arcade at Billingham in Durham, and the
thirteenth century arcades at Tytherington in
Gloucestershire consist of arches with large masses

of the earlier wall left between them. Such a
method was economical, as much less dressed stone
was required; and we find it employed at Copford
in Essex, where good building stone was hard to get.
Nevertheless, it prevented the free circulation of
light from the windows of the aisles, and practically
shut off the aisles from the church.

§ 44.   There is one obvious consequence of the
setting out of aisles on either side of an existing
building which, although an imperfection in itself,
contributes greatly to the variety of the parish
church plan. The builders cannot see both their
aisles at one and the same time : the older church
comes in between.   In fact, until the nave and aisles
are actually joined, at the close of the work, by the
breaking down of the walls beneath the arches, there
can be no opportunity of appreciating the full effect
of the work.   There is a famous instance at Beverley
minster of the mistakes to which the presence of the
older building may lead. The aisles of the nave were
set out in the fourteenth century on either side of an
older and shorter nave.   The south aisle was set out
first, the width of the eastern bay being measured
from a new buttress in the angle of nave and transept.
On the north side there was a thirteenth century
buttress in this position : the builders, in setting out
their north aisle, overlooked the fact that this buttress
was of less projection than the newly built one on

the other side, with the result that their buttress measurements throughout varied on both sides, while the standard of width between the buttresses, which had been employed on the south side, was retained. Consequently, as the columns, in a vaulted church, have to be built in line with the buttresses of the corresponding aisle walls, the columns were not opposite one another, and the discrepancy increased as the church advanced westward. When the builders got clear of the intervening building, in the western bays of the nave, they were able to rectify their mistake slightly; but the effect is unpleasantly noticeable in the obliquity of the transverse arches of the vaulting.

§ 45. If errors like this could take place in churches where the width of the bays of the aisles was calculated, they were much more likely to take place where builders worked with less accurate ideas of measurement. In an unvaulted church, where the pressure of the roof is not a serious factor in the construction, the exact correspondence of pier to buttress need not be taken into account; and there are many churches in which the spacing of the aisles is quite independent of that of the arcades. This happens at Melbourne, where the church was not planned for stone vaulting. The builders seem to have thought that they could get in six bays between the transept and the space planned for

one of the western towers ; but found that, on the
measurements they had adopted, there was room
only for five. They corrected their miscalculation
by broadening the division of the wall between the
fourth and fifth bay of the aisles. When they came
to build the arcades, they were conscious of their
previous error, and planned them in five equal bays
irrespective of the plan of the aisles. In churches of
the fourteenth and fifteenth centuries, especially in
districts like Norfolk or south Lincolnshire, where
much rebuilding was done, the regularity of plan is
often remarkable. The nave of the famous church of
Heckington, near Sleaford, was planned with an exact
correspondence between aisles and arcades: pier
is opposite buttress, window opposite window. Islip
and Brampton Ash in Northamptonshire show an equal
accuracy. But, while such agreement is desirable, it
is neither necessary nor general. And, where the
arcades are broken through earlier walls, the correspondence is seldom very precise. The central line
of the east walls of the aisles, as set out first, will
usually correspond to a line drawn across the centre
of the chancel arch : similarly, the line of the west
walls will be an extension of the west wall of the
nave, or of a line drawn across the tower arch. The
aisles will be spaced into as many equal, or nearly
equal bays, as can be got in between the buttresses
at either end. When, however, the building of the

arcade is taken in hand, the responds or half-piers at either end will seldom be built directly against the piers of the chancel arch, or against the west wall of the nave ; but projecting pieces of the old walls will be left as a backing to them. It follows that, although the arcade may be divided into the same number of bays as the aisles, the standard of spacing will be different, and consequently, unless a very regular system of planning is adopted, the piers will not be exactly opposite the solid portions of the aisle walls, and consequently the centres of the arches will be out of line with the centres of the windows. Again, it may be that, by accident or design, the backing for the responds may project more on one side of the nave than on the other, at either or both ends. The result will be that the piers of one arcade will be out of line with those of the arcade opposite. That discrepancies of this kind were sometimes the result of intention cannot be denied ; but there is generally some practical reason to be found for the intention, and the discrepancies themselves were a *pis aller* which the builders would have avoided, if they could. That deliberate irregularity with which medieval masons are sometimes credited is a fancy, which careful consideration of the circumstances will dispel.

§ 46. Hitherto we have spoken of the aisled nave as though both aisles were planned at one and the same time. This, however, was by no means always

the case.   At Gretton in Northamptonshire, the
north aisle was built soon after the beginning of the
twelfth century : the south aisle followed twenty or
thirty years later.   The north arcade at Northallerton
is of massive twelfth century work, with rounded
arches : the south arcade was added in the thirteenth
century, and has slender columns with pointed arches.
In such cases, the north aisle may have been built first,
to avoid interference with the burial ground south of
the church.   Very often only one aisle was added.   The
little church of Whitwell, Rutland, has a south aisle,
added in the fourteenth century, with a chapel at its
east end.   No north aisle was built : but a drain in the
north wall of the nave shows that there was a third
altar against the north side of the rood screen.
Usually, when one aisle was built long after another,
the spacing of the new arcade was made to correspond
with that of the old.   If the old arcade had heavy
twelfth century columns, the new one, with its lighter
columns, would have broader arches.   But it sometimes happens that the old spacing was disregarded,
for very good reasons.   The north arcade of Middleton
Tyas church, in north Yorkshire, consists of six bays :
the columns are heavy, the arches low and round
headed, and very narrow.   The interior of the church
must have been very dark ; and the builders of the
south aisle, in the fourteenth century, aimed at
throwing more light upon it.   They therefore planned

their new arcade, with broad pointed arches springing
from octagonal columns, in four instead of six bays,
and so, from broad windows in the aisle, introduced
the necessary light. Something of the same kind
happened at Theddingworth in Leicestershire : the
effect is, of course, one-sided, but in both cases the
light admitted enhances the merits of the earlier
arcade, which, until then, had to be taken on trust.

§ 47. But there are further instances—and these,
perhaps, are the most instructive—where aisles were
not merely built at two different periods, but where
the growth of one or both aisles was gradual. As an
instance of this, may be cited the beautiful church
of Raunds in Northamptonshire. Raunds seems to
have been one of those cases in which the Norman
chancel and nave were of the same width, and possibly
were undivided by any chancel arch. In the thirteenth century the west tower and spire were built,
and a broad south aisle was added to the nave. This
aisle was of four bays, and the point at which it
stopped probably marked the dividing line between
the nave and chancel. However, the builders certainly intended to carry on the aisle eastward, as a
south chapel to the chancel, which they now rebuilt
and lengthened. Early in the fourteenth century,
the south aisle was continued eastward, an arcade
of five bays being added to the four bays already
existing. The new bays were made rather narrower

than those in the earlier part of the arcade. A
strange feature of the new work was the insertion of
a chancel arch, the south pier of which bisects one of
the new arches. Thus, while three bays and a half of
the new arcade belong to the chancel and quire, a
bay and a half belong to the nave. The arch dividing
the south aisle from the chancel chapel springs from

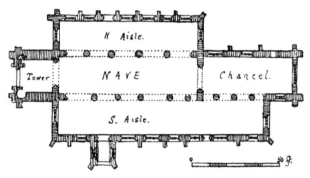

Fig. 10. Plan of Raunds church, Northants.

the pier between the end of the old arcade and the
inserted pier of the chancel arch. At the same time,
the outer wall of the south aisle seems to have been
practically rebuilt, although much of the older work
was retained. There may have been a thirteenth
century north aisle as well. Whether this was the
case or no, a new north aisle and arcade were built

during the fourteenth century. The aisle was set
out in seven bays, six of which contained broad
three-light windows, while a north doorway was made
in the third bay from the west end. The east wall
was built on foundations in a line with the chancel
arch, while the west wall was in a line with the tower
arch and west wall of the south aisle. It is obvious,
therefore, that the planning of the new aisle was
totally different from that of the older aisle and
chapel. However, when the builders came to their
arcade, instead of building it in seven bays, as the new
aisle demanded, they built it in five, setting their new
columns in a line with those on the opposite side.
But while, on the south side, there was an awkward
half-bay between the end of the arcade and the
chancel arch, a solid piece of wall was left between
the north pier of the chancel arch and the eastern
respond of the new arcade. A compromise was thus
effected between the aisles, and an appearance of
regularity was ensured. Directly, however, one
begins to examine the plan of the church, and to
trace the transverse lines from window to window,
and buttress to buttress, it will be found that only in
one place can a line be drawn which will pass straight
from the centre of one buttress to that of the buttress
opposite, and will pass through the centre of the
intervening columns on its way.

§ 48. It already has been shown that builders

were very unwilling, in making their additions to
churches, to destroy old work altogether. At times
they displayed an extraordinary conservatism in their
re-use of old material in their new work. This was
not invariable. In the splendid churches of south
Lincolnshire, during the fourteenth century, their
aim seems to have been complete rebuilding; and
such examples as the magnificent nave at Swaton,
near Sleaford, or the neighbouring church of Billing-
borough, show how old work must have been swept
away by the enthusiasm for lofty arcades, elaborately
traceried windows, and walls of dressed stone-work.
On the other hand, half the charm of the hardly less
beautiful churches of Northamptonshire is the result
of the clever way in which the masons dove-tailed all
the old stone-work which was worth preserving into
their new additions. Such churches as Tansor and
Oundle are, for that reason, unexcelled in interest,
offering, as they do, almost inexhaustible problems
as to the development of their plan. In all parts of
England we find that builders, whatever else they
destroyed, carefully kept, as a general rule, the
doorways, and especially the south doorway, of the
buildings which they enlarged. This accounts for
the large number of handsome Norman doorways
which remain in the walls of aisles obviously later than
the doorways themselves. At Birkin in Yorkshire,
the south aisle was not built till the middle of the

fourteenth century, but the doorway was removed to its new position from the wall of the aisleless church. One very exceptional case occurs at Felton in Northumberland. Towards the beginning of the thirteenth century, the west part of the south wall of the church was cut through, a chapel was added, and, east of the chapel, a porch was built. Rather more than fifty or sixty years later, it was determined to add a south aisle the full length of the nave. The width of the aisle was taken from that of the existing chapel and porch. To connect the chapel with the new work, the side walls of the porch were cut through. The outer doorway of the porch became the new south doorway, while the inner doorway was kept unaltered, as an arch in the new arcade.

§ 49. Features which have been touched upon in connexion with Raunds bring us to two new features in the plan—the rebuilding of aisles and the lengthening of churches westward. In most parish churches, aisles, when they were added at first, were extremely narrow. The west wall of Hallaton church in Leicestershire, for example, shows that, in the fourteenth century, originally narrow aisles were heightened and widened. The roof lines of the earlier aisles remain : they were clearly under the same roof as the nave of the church, and had very low side walls. This was not always the case. At Raunds the thirteenth century south aisle was always broad and lofty, and must have had its own roof from the first. And, as the principles of Gothic construction became more familiar, and the larger churches began to exercise a more wide-spread influence upon the parish church, aisles began to increase in breadth and elevation. The small and narrow windows of churches of the twelfth and early thirteenth centuries gave way to the broad mullioned and traceried windows of fully developed Gothic work. For these, with their advantage of increased light, more head-way was necessary. Aisle walls were consequently heightened or altogether rebuilt. The acutely pointed roof of the nave could no longer be con-tinued downwards to cover these higher aisles. The aisle was consequently covered with a lean-to roof, or with a separate gabled roof of its own. A free increase in width was thus possible. The church of Appleton-le-Street in Yorkshire has a short nave with north and south aisles. The north aisle, added in the early part of the thirteenth century, is narrow, and the roof of the nave was continued over it. The south aisle, which was probably rebuilt a little before 1300, is broader and has a separate lean-to roof. The wide east window of this aisle could not have been introduced, had the south aisle been built to match the scale of the north aisle.

§ 50. The introduction of more light, however, was not the only reason for the rebuilding and

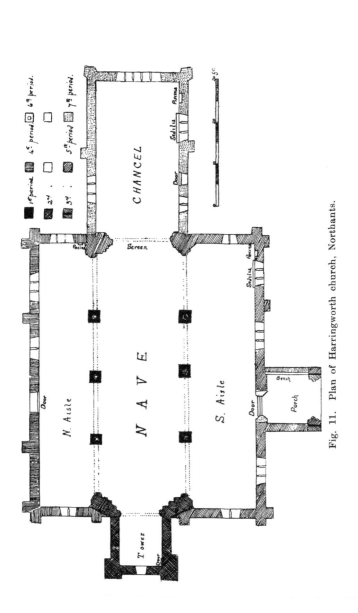

Fig. 11. Plan of Harringworth church, Northants.

heightening of aisles. The east end of an aisle, as has
been said, provided a convenient place for one of the
side altars of the church. This was the case even
in the narrow aisles of the twelfth and thirteenth
century, many of which, like the north aisle of Great
Easton church in Leicestershire, provided with a
drain, aumbry, or a corbel for a statue, bear witness
to the existence of a contemporary altar. At
Harringworth in Northamptonshire there had been
an aisleless church, to which a tower had been added
at the end of the twelfth, and aisles early in the
thirteenth century. On 24 October 1305 Edward I
granted letters patent to William la Zouche, by
which he had licence to assign a certain amount of
land to two chantry chaplains in the chapel of All
Saints. This may have been his private chapel,
but was possibly in the church. A little earlier than
this, to judge by the character of the architecture, a
new north aisle had been built, with a new altar at
the east end. Very soon after the granting of the
licence, it would appear that the whole of the south
arcade was taken down, and a new south aisle and
arcade built. The work was done in a very con-
servative spirit, for the old thirteenth century porch
and inner doorway were rebuilt on the new site, and
an old string-course was re-used internally, beneath
the new windows. The piscina and the three sedilia,
which belonged to the altar at the end of the aisle,

remain in the south wall, and there are corbels for
statues on either side of the east window. However,
rebuilding did not stop here ; for it seems that,
during the next few years, the north arcade was
entirely rebuilt so as nearly to match that on the
south. Thus the work, beginning with the north
aisle, and extending over some thirty or forty years,
finished on the side on which it began. Numerous
examples of a closely parallel kind, fortified by
documentary evidence, might be given.

§ 51. The rebuilding of the south aisle, about
1313, at Newark, was the prelude to an entire rebuilding of the church, which extended over many
years. The builders began by setting out their aisles
as usual, and by the middle of the fourteenth century
the south aisle was finished, and the lower courses of
the north aisle and the new aisled chancel were built.
However, in 1349, the Black Death interrupted the
work. The north aisle and chancel were not
completed, and the new arcades of nave and
chancel were not built until the fifteenth century.
In this case there were certainly older, and almost
certainly narrower aisles. The rebuilding included
aisles on a larger scale, and new internal arcades
whose spacing corresponded to the spacing of the
aisle walls. All systematic rebuilding, in the full
development of Gothic art, began with the planning
of the aisles. The naves of Cirencester and North-

leach churches, rebuilt at the end of the middle
ages, are examples of this method. The arcades at

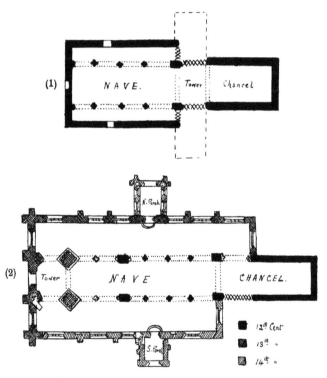

Fig. 12. Plans of Grantham church : (1) probable arrangement
about 1190; (2) at beginning of 14th century.

Cirencester are known to have been built about
1514-5; but the aisles were obviously completed
first, and their remodelling may have been begun
in the second quarter of the fifteenth century. At
Northleach the nave was finished about 1458; and
there seems to have been a break of some years
between the building of the aisles and the destruction
of the older church which, no doubt, lay within them.
But it did not always happen that the full intention
of the builders was carried out. One of the most
splendid schemes which we possess for the enlargement
of a parish church was the great enterprise begun
at Grantham soon after the middle of the thirteenth
century. An aisleless Norman church had been enlarged at the end of the twelfth century by the addition
of aisles to the nave, the connexion being formed
by arcades of rounded arches springing from very
elegant clustered columns. Above the arcades were
low clerestories, lighted by round-headed windows.
About 1230, the neighbouring church of Newark
was taken in hand by masons, who built a new west
tower up to a certain height, and, as an afterthought,
planned aisles to engage the tower completely. As
we have seen, the building of the aisles at Newark
upon their present scale did not begin till much later.
The work of rebuilding at Grantham was clearly
inspired by that already begun at Newark. A tower
was planned on a site much to the west of the nave,

and was engaged within very broad aisles. The tower
and north aisle were set out first. The north aisle
was divided into seven bays, with a large traceried
window in each bay, the western bay being much
wider between the buttresses than the rest, owing to
the greater space taken up by the tower and its piers
internally. The remaining six bays were set out
with equal widths between the buttresses, the middle
bay of the aisle being covered by a porch. The
eastern bay overlapped the western part of the
aisleless chancel, its western buttress being in a line
with the division between chancel and nave. The
western bay of the south aisle was set out about the
same time, and there was, no doubt, an intention of
proceeding with the rest on the same lines as in the
north aisle. There can also be little doubt that the
builders intended to take down the old arcades, and
build new arcades, with spacing corresponding to
that of their aisles, and to lengthen the chancel
eastwards, while bringing its western portion into
the nave. The tower and north aisle were built on
the intended scale ; and, when the tower had risen to
a certain height, the ambition of the builders was
fired to add to it an extra stage, hitherto uncon-
templated, below the spire with which it was to be
crowned. This project of giving their church a tower
and stone spire, which remained, for many years,
the loftiest in England, evidently curtailed the full

accomplishment of their earlier plan. The columns
of the old arcades were kept, and the tower was
connected by arcades of two bays with the angles of
the west wall of the old church ; while an arch was
pierced through the north wall of the chancel, to give
access to the east bay of the new aisle. The new
arches were pointed : in order to match them, the
older round-headed arches were taken down, and
pointed arches built, which cut into and blocked the
clerestory windows. This change was made with
great economy of material, the springing stones of
some of the old arches being kept to afford footing
for the new. When the south aisle was seriously
begun, about 1300, similar economy was shown.
Four bays, in addition to the western bay, were
spaced out, without regard to the plan of the north
aisle. The fourth bay from the west was covered by
a porch, smaller than that on the north side ; and the
east wall of the aisle was probably built on a line
with the division between nave and chancel. Half a
century later, the east wall was taken down, and the
south aisle was extended to the full length of the
chancel ; but this later development was not contemplated by the thirteenth century builders. These
hesitations and changes, consequent upon the expense
entailed by the north aisle and by the alteration in
the elevation of the tower and spire, make Grantham
second to no English church in interest.

§ 52. Grantham also provides us with a lengthened nave. The position of its earlier west wall is
clearly shown by the masses of masonry which
occur between the eastern bay of the new, and
western bay of the old, arcade on either side. The
responds on the eastern side of these pieces of wall
are twelfth century work : on the west side, they
belong to the later part of the thirteenth century.
Such lengthening was probably very common in later
Gothic times, and we may surmise that it took place
in many instances where arcades were entirely rebuilt, and no visible trace of the process was left.
However, there are many churches in which one or
more extra bays have been added to the nave, and
the join of the old and new work is marked as at
Grantham. Whaplode church in south Lincolnshire
had its early twelfth century nave lengthened by three
bays about 1180. At Colsterworth, near Grantham,
a western bay was added to the nave about the same
time, and an earlier north aisle lengthened. Above
the piece of wall which occurs between the older and
newer work, the quoins of the aisleless church remain
entire. Usually, as at Grantham, the lengthening of
the nave was undertaken in connexion with a new
western tower, which was built up outside the church,
and then connected with it by one or two bays of
arcading. Almost contemporary with the tower and
spire of Grantham are those of Tilney All Saints, near

Lynn. Here a single bay was added west of the late twelfth century nave; and, as no new aisles were contemplated, the old arcades, with their rounded arches, were left intact. Bubwith in Yorkshire, and

Fig. 13. Gretton, Northants: extension of 12th century arcade to meet 15th century tower.

Caunton in Nottinghamshire, are later examples of churches where the tower was built west of the end of an earlier nave, and a bay was built to connect it with the older work. Sometimes, as at Gretton in

Northamptonshire, where the slope of a steep hill
forbade extension far to the west, a new tower was
built only a few feet beyond the limit of the old nave.
In such a case, the side walls of the nave might be
carried solid westwards to meet the tower, or, as
happened at Gretton, narrow arches might be made
between the tower and the west end of the older
wall.   The beautiful tower and spire at Oundle were
built just outside the west wall of the thirteenth
century nave ; and were doubtless intended to be
followed by a complete rebuilding of the arcades—
such a rebuilding as took place at Lavenham in
Suffolk, towards the end of the fifteenth century.
The idea, however, was abandoned, and the space
between the arcades and the tower filled in solid with
rather rough masonry.

§ 53.   The position of the western tower in the
plan is normally at the west end of the nave, with
which it is connected by an arch, low at first, but
loftier as time goes on, until, in later Gothic churches,
its height frequently is nearly that of the whole nave.
The remaining three walls are usually external, and
clear of the aisles.   But sometimes, owing to a freak
of planning, or, more frequently, owing to the con-
ditions of the site, the tower is, as at Bibury, at the
west end of one of the aisles.   At Gedling in
Nottinghamshire the tower and spire are at the
end of the north aisle.   The tower of St Michael's,

Cambridge, is at the west end of the south aisle :
probably the western extension of the church was
prevented by the neighbourhood of the street, a
circumstance which often accounts for the irregularity
of plan in some town churches. At St Mary Redcliffe,
Bristol, built on the edge of the "red cliff" from which
it takes its name, the tower and spire are at the end
of the north aisle : had they been planned in the
usual place, a full bay of the nave would have been
sacrificed. The tower at Spalding was planned, in
the first instance, to stand against the south wall of
the west bay of the south aisle : subsequently a new
south aisle was built east of it. One of the most
curious instances is that of St Mary's at Leicester,
where the tower, subsequently, as at Spalding,
heightened by a spire, was planned in the thirteenth
century, outside a very narrow south aisle. A tower
at the west end of the nave would have encroached
upon the inner ward of the adjacent castle. The
chancel of St Mary's was used for collegiate services,
and parochial accommodation was limited. Towards
the end of the thirteenth century, a very wide south
aisle, a parish church in itself, was built the full length
of the nave, and overlapping the chancel at the east
end. The tower was left standing on piers entirely
within the west end of the new aisle. It may be
added that, where towers occur at the end of aisles,
they seldom project beyond the west wall of the nave,

but open into the nave by an arch in the north or
south wall, as the case may be. Plans with two
western towers, as at Melbourne or St Margaret's at
Lynn, are of very rare occurrence ; and, where they
are found, the plan was probably designed on more
ambitious lines than those of the ordinary parish
church.

§ 54. The plan in which the western tower is
engaged within the aisles—that is, where the aisles
are brought up flush with the west end of the church—
is not very common. Still, instances occur in all
parts of England. At Grantham, the plan is deliberate. It was imitated, as has been said, from
Newark, where the side walls of the tower had been
pierced with arches as an after-thought. Newark, in
turn, may have taken the design from Tickhill in
south Yorkshire ; and the design at Tickhill may
have been taken from the early and unpretentious
example at Sherburn-in-Elmet. Grantham probably
suggested other similar designs, such as Ewerby, near
Sleaford. Several of our finest late Gothic churches,
like St Nicholas at Newcastle, have plans in which
the aisles are continued up to the west face of the
tower. The method affords full development to the
aisles, and, as at Sileby in Leicestershire, has an
imposing interior effect. Outside, however, the aisles
crowd the base of the tower too much, and the fine
effect of a lofty, free standing tower is lost. Some-

times aisles were extended westwards, so as to engage
an earlier tower, as at Sleaford, where the low tower and
spire are almost overwhelmed by a pair of wide fourteenth century aisles. At Brigstock and Winterton,
late Saxon towers have been left without alteration
inside aisles which have been brought westward in
the thirteenth and fourteenth centuries. The nave of
Holy Trinity, Cambridge, was much widened in the
fourteenth century, and a small tower and spire of
earlier date were brought entirely within the new
nave, as happened in the south aisle at St Mary's,
Leicester, and were left without sufficient abutment.
As a consequence, the arches of the ground story
had to be strengthened about a century later with
additional masonry. Cases occur, as at Coln Rogers
in Gloucestershire, where a tower has been built
within the west end of an earlier church. In most of
such instances, the churchyard boundary probably
allowed of no further building westward. The near-
ness of the churchyard boundary also seems to have
given cause to a peculiarity which may be seen at
Wollaton, near Nottingham, Dedham in Essex, and
in a few other places, where the west tower is in its
usual position, but is pierced from north to south by
an archway. It is possible that this gave facility to
processions, which could thus pass round the church
without leaving consecrated ground The tower of
old All Saints, Cambridge, now destroyed, projected

over the public foot-way of the street, which passed
through its ground story ; while St John's, Bristol, is
built on the city wall, and the tower and spire, which
it shared with the adjoining church of St Lawrence,
are over the south gate of the city.

§ 55.   Sometimes, as at Oundle, the tower was
rebuilt with a view to the reconstruction of the
whole church.   But, as also at Oundle, the design was
often abandoned, or was altered.   The magnificent
tower of St Michael's, Coventry, was built, between
1373 and 1394, at the west end of an older nave :
its spire was not begun till 1430.   Whether the
rebuilding of the nave was contemplated when the
tower was begun, it is impossible to say.   A new
nave was actually begun in 1432, and finished in 1450.
A thoroughfare immediately south of the church
prevented extension on that side.   The old south
porch was retained in place as the principal entrance,
so that the line of the wall of the south aisle follows
closely that of the original church.   The new south
arcade was set out, not in a line with the south-east
buttress of the tower, but somewhat to the north of
it, so that the buttress is external ; while, for the
width of the nave, a space approximating to twice the
internal breadth of the tower was taken.   The tower
is thus placed almost wholly south of the central
axis of the nave produced westward.   Here, once
more, we may note the influence of site on the plan.

§ 56. The people's entrance to the church was
ordinarily through a porch, covering the north or
south doorway of the nave. The south doorway is
usually covered by a porch. Frequently, as at Hallaton
in Leicestershire, or Henbury in Gloucestershire, there
is a north as well as a south porch. At Warmington,
near Oundle, where there is a beautiful doorway in
the west tower, the vaulted south porch is the
principal entrance ; but there is also a somewhat
smaller north porch, also vaulted. The chief porch
at Grantham is on the north side ; but there is also a
large porch on the south. At Newark, there is only
a south porch, on the side of the church next the
market place. The south porch of St Mary Redcliffe,
at Bristol, is the ordinary entrance of the church ; but
the chief entrance of the building, until the fifteenth
century, was on the north side, at the head of the
abrupt slope towards the city. In the fourteenth
century, this entrance was covered by a large and
lofty octagonal porch, approached by a flight of steps.
There is an octagonal south porch at Chipping Norton,
and a hexagonal south porch at Ludlow. The magnificent porches of the fifteenth century, as at Burford
in Oxfordshire, Northleach in Gloucestershire, Worstead in Norfolk, Walberswick in Suffolk, St Mary
Magdalene's at Taunton, or Yatton in Somerset, are
usually on the south side of the church.

§ 57. The positions of the porch and doorway in

7—2

the wall of the aisle vary. At St Nicholas, Newcastle,
where the west tower is engaged within the aisles,
there is a porch in the western bay of each aisle.
Usually, however, the porch will be found in the
second bay of one of the aisles, counting from the
west end. Sometimes, especially in larger churches,
the porch occurs a bay further east. At Warmington
and at Grantham, the two porches of either church
are nearly opposite each other, and project approximately from the centre of the walls of the aisles.
Where the porch has been pushed eastward in this
way, the west end of the aisle seems to have been
occupied by one or more chapels. There are indications of this at Warmington ; while, in the neighbouring church of Tansor, where the porch is in the
usual place, but the aisle has been lengthened somewhat to the west, there was certainly an altar west,
as well as east, of the porch. There was at least one
chantry chapel west of the south porch at Grantham.
The south porch at Ludlow covers the wall of the
third bay of the aisle from the west : here there were
two chapels in the western part of the aisle. There
was another chapel at the west end of the north aisle.
It can hardly be proved that the position of porches
was actually planned with this use of the aisles in
view ; but there can be no doubt that advantage was
frequently taken of the space thus added to the aisle.

CHAPTER V

II. Transepts and Chancel

§ 58.   The aisled nave, with its usual appendages
of porch and tower, has now been described at length.
Before we proceed to the development of the chancel,
the transepts or transeptal chapels of the parish
church invite discussion.   The distinction between
true transepts, in churches with central towers, and
the transeptal chapels which are nothing more than
northern and southern extensions of the aisles, has
been made already; and it has been seen that the
cruciform plan with central tower reached a very full
state of perfection during the twelfth century.   Further
dignity was given to some cruciform churches by the
addition of aisles to the transepts.   St Mary Redcliffe
at Bristol, the plan of which is that of a large collegiate
or cathedral rather than a parish church, has transepts
with eastern and western aisles: there is no central
tower, but the transepts form a definite cross-arm to
the church, which was designed with regard to the

central point formed by the crossing of a longitudinal
and a transverse axis. There are few churches in
England as beautiful as that of Melton Mowbray,
with its aisled transepts and tower above the crossing:
had the chancel only been planned on a larger scale
and with aisles, the unrivalled beauty and dignity of
St Mary Redcliffe might have been approached here.
The cruciform plan with central tower is the most
noble of all church plans, when carried out by builders
with large ideas. Churches like Ludlow, Nantwich,
Holy Trinity and St John's at Coventry, St Mary's at
Beverley, excite an admiration which is the natural
result of the fact that the plan, instead of straggling
in the ordinary way from east to west, is brought to
a focus beneath the central tower.

§ 59. Apart, however, from the tower above the
crossing, the transept had a value of its own. It gave
additional room for the side altars of the church. The
transeptal chapels at Worth allowed of greater width
for the chancel arch: the altars, which naturally
would have stood against the wall on either side of
the chancel arch, could be placed within these excrescences from the north and south walls of the
church, and the central space was thus left clear.
This method of extension of the church by adding
north and south chapels to the nave was pursued
throughout the middle ages. The thirteenth century
plan of Acton Burnell is virtually identical with the

tenth or eleventh century plan of Worth. In aisled
churches, such transeptal additions are simply out-
growths of the aisle walls, and were not necessarily
planned with any regard to the spacing of the arcades
of the nave. . They may, of course, be placed symmetrically at the east end of the aisles, the width of each

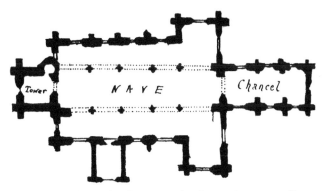

Fig. 14.   Plan of 13th century church : west tower, south
porch, unequal transeptal chapels.

chapel corresponding to the width of the arch of the
arcade which is opposite its opening. Thus Exton
church in Rutland, rebuilt about the beginning of the
thirteenth century, has north and south transeptal
chapels whose width is that of the eastern bay of each
arcade. A transverse arch was thrown across each
aisle at its junction with the adjacent chapel. Here

the chapels form quasi-transepts in perfect union with
the design of nave and aisles. Symmetrical plans in
which it is clear at a glance that the transeptal chapels
are developments of the aisles, and have no necessary
relation to the nave, are those of Kegworth in
Leicestershire, rebuilt in the fourteenth century, and
Aylsham, Cawston, and Sall in Norfolk, which belong
to the fifteenth century. But even more obvious than
these are the plans in which transeptal chapels have
been thrown out at different periods, or even at one
and the same period, without the least regard to
symmetry. A small aisleless nave at Stretton in
Rutland received a north aisle about the beginning of
the thirteenth century. Soon after, the eastern part
of the side walls was taken down, and chapels built
out to north and south. The width of the south
chapel was determined by that of the old chancel arch,
which was rebuilt between the chapel and the nave,
there being no aisle on that side. The north chapel,
on the other hand, was formed simply by returning
the wall of the aisle northward, and throwing a transverse arch across the aisle from the wall above the
arcade. Its width corresponds roughly with that of
the south chapel, but has no correspondence with
that of the adjacent bay of the arcade. Examples of
this form of growth of plan, dictated by convenience
and the necessity of the moment, are common in every
part of England.

§ 60. It is quite clear that the transeptal chapel, being nothing more than an excrescence from the wall of a nave or aisle, is a feature which may be treated with some freedom. Its width and length are dependent upon the convenience and will of the builders. The north chapel of the aisleless church of Clapton-in-Gordano, Somerset, is entered by an arch in the east part of the north wall : the chapel itself, however, extends some distance westward, so that its longer axis is parallel to the longer axis of the nave. The south chapel, again, at Lowick in Northamptonshire has its longer axis from east to west, although its roof is at right angles to that of the adjacent aisle. Externally, its transeptal character is apparent; internally, it has the appearance of an additional south aisle. A chantry was founded in this chapel in 1498. Very often, where special chantry chapels were built, they took the position of transeptal chapels. Cases in point are the late Gothic chantry chapels in All Saints and St Lawrence's at Evesham. Such chapels may obviously be lengthened westward, like the chapel at Clapton-in-Gordano, so that they become additional aisles. The Milcombe chapel at Bloxham in Oxfordshire, the Greenway aisle at Tiverton in Devonshire, and the side chapels of the north and south aisles at St Andrew's, Plymouth, and Plympton St Mary are the logical outcome of the habit of adding transeptal chapels to the plan. Two transeptal chapels of the ordinary type are found in other Devonshire churches rebuilt in the fifteenth century, as at East Portlemouth : the Kirkham chapel at Paignton, famous for its carved stone-work, is transeptal. From this it is but a step to the chapels at Plymouth and Plympton, with their longer axes from east to west : while the aisle at Tiverton (1517) develops naturally, in the churches of Cullompton (1526) and Ottery St Mary (before 1530), into a vaulted aisle the full length of the nave. At Bloxham, on the other hand, the Milcombe chapel, which extends from the east wall of the south aisle as far as the porch, was probably grafted upon an earlier and smaller transeptal chapel. A comparison with the neighbouring church of Adderbury shows that the fabric of the transeptal chapels at Adderbury is largely of the twelfth century. The north chapel at Bloxham is, in its present state, much later ; but the similarity of plan to that of Adderbury leads to the justifiable conclusion that it was rebuilt on old foundations, and that there was a similar south chapel. About 1290 the aisles at Bloxham were widened, and a beautiful arcade of two bays was built at the east end of the north aisle, between it and the north chapel. Within the next few years, the aisles at Adderbury were also widened, and arcades similar to that at Bloxham, though coarser in detail, were built at the east end of either aisle. The projection of the transeptal chapels from the side walls was now very slight; and, in the fifteenth century, the projection of the south chapel at Bloxham was absorbed by the building of the Milcombe chapel, between which and the south aisle an arcade of two bays was made. There is more intrinsic interest in this gradual development of plan than in the Devonshire plans we have noticed, which are all due to fifteenth century rebuildings; and the mutual influence exercised throughout the middle ages by two neighbouring churches like Bloxham and Adderbury gives us an insight into the progress of local art which the energy of fifteenth century masons in certain districts has somewhat obscured. From the arrangement of the south transept at Adderbury, there appear to have been two altars in each of the chapels.

§ 61. Transeptal chapels occasionally appear in unusual positions. For example, at Branscombe in south Devon, there is a tower between nave and chancel. There are, however, no transepts; but transeptal chapels are built out from the walls of the aisleless nave, west of the tower. These chapels appear to be enlargements of earlier transeptal chapels; while the tower seems to have been built over the chancel of the earlier church. Heckington church in south Lincolnshire was rebuilt in the fourteenth century. The nave has aisles with transeptal chapels, very regular and symmetrical in plan, but is continued beyond the opening of the transeptal projections by an aisleless bay, east of which comes the chancel arch. At Bottesford in north Lincolnshire, where much rebuilding was done in the thirteenth century, the transeptal chapels open from the bay east of the chancel arch. In the case of Heckington, the earlier church was probably cruciform : when the rebuilding came to pass, the ground plan of the western portion of the church was kept, while the chancel was built on an extended plan, and the site of the western part of the old chancel thrown into the nave. The case of Bottesford is probably accounted for in the opposite way : the site was not enlarged eastwards, but the chancel was lengthened by the absorption of the eastern part of the old nave.

§ 62. There are a number of cases in which transeptal chapels have been kept from an earlier cruciform plan, in which they may have formed true transepts. The fine church of Oundle, whose western tower and spire already have been mentioned as built about 1400, has very fully developed transeptal chapels. The nave and aisles, and the greater part of the chapels, are, in their present state, work of the thirteenth century ; but the eastern bay of the present nave was entirely remodelled about 1350, when a clerestory was added. This bay had evidently been designed to carry a central tower : the nave arcades stop west of it, and there is a thick piece of wall between them

and the arches opening from it into the chapels.
These arches and the chancel arch were entirely
reconstructed at the time just mentioned. The
western arch, however, was removed, and an original
crossing was thus converted into a bay of the nave.
Whether there ever was a central tower is, of course,
an uncertain point ; but the building of a west tower
on a new site not many years after this reconstruction
is a fact which makes the previous existence of a
central tower probable. The removal of a central
tower would be due to one of two causes. Either
its supports were weak, or it blocked up the space
between nave and chancel too much. The central
tower of Petersfield in Hampshire was taken down ;
but its east wall still remains between nave and
chancel. However, if there are cases in which a
central tower was removed, and a west tower built,
there are probably more in which a central tower was
planned, and then abandoned. Campsall church,
near Doncaster, has unmistakable signs of a projected
cruciform plan with a central tower, and has a regular
crossing with transepts. But it is probable that the
builders changed their minds before the nave was
finished ; and, although they doubtless left the arches,
which were intended to bear their tower, for a later
generation to remove and rebuild, they went westward
and built a tower at the other end of the nave. This
tower was finished towards the end of the third

quarter of the twelfth century. The builders of
Newark church, who were peculiarly susceptible to
after-thoughts, apparently planned a central tower in
the later part of the twelfth century. It is difficult to
explain otherwise the slender clusters of shafts which
project into the nave from the first pier west of the
chancel arch on either side. Such piers were hardly
capable of bearing the weight of a tower ; and so the
builders must have thought. Early in the thirteenth
century, they began the present west tower, the first
stage of a rebuilding which, with long intervals,
continued into the sixteenth century. The final step
by which the church reached its present plan was the
addition of a transeptal chapel to either aisle, opposite
the site which, more than three centuries before, had
been chosen for the piers of the abandoned central
tower.

§ 63. Even in strictly cruciform churches, transepts were sometimes treated with a freedom which
was more appropriate to the transeptal chapel. It is
not unusual to find one transept longer than the other,
as at Felmersham in Bedfordshire. Here, however,
the transepts are not only of different lengths, but the
south transept is loftier, as well as shorter, than the
north, which is little more than a chapel-like excrescence from the tower. At Witney in Oxfordshire
both transepts are of great projection, but the north
transept is slightly longer than that on the south.

Fig. 15. St Mary's, Beverley : arcades of quire and
S. transept, from S.W.

Both have considerable traces of thirteenth century work ; but, in the fourteenth century, the north transept was lengthened by an addition divided into two stories, the upper of which was a chapel, while the lower was probably a vaulted bone-hole. The south transept was also lengthened ; and a chapel was built, projecting from its east wall near the south end. Both transepts have western aisles : that of the north transept, which stops short of the two-storied extension, contained an altar near the north end. There are traces of at least three other altars in the transepts, so that there was excellent reason for their somewhat unusual projection. At St Mary's, Beverley, an eastern aisle was added to the south transept in the fifteenth century, to provide more room for altars. The north transept already had a large chapel of two stages upon its eastern side, so that the plan was treated unsymmetrically. The tower of St Mary's at Stafford rests on heavy piers and narrow arches, and is flanked by north and south transepts. However, while the south transept, of good thirteenth century work, is rather small and short, the north transept was rebuilt with great magnificence in the fourteenth century, and its internal effect is that of a large side chapel rather than a transept. Aisled transepts are never common, even in large churches. Instances in which a tran-septal chapel is aisled are even less common. The

aisled south chapel at Medbourne in Leicestershire
has been mentioned in an earlier chapter. Oakham
and Langham churches in Rutland have large transeptal chapels with western aisles : the north chapel
at Langham was removed in the fifteenth century,
when the aisles of the nave were widened.

§ 64. Reference has also been made to those
plans in which the side walls of a tower between
chancel and nave have been pierced with arches, and
quasi-transepts have been constructed. This is very
noticeable at Almondsbury in Gloucestershire, where
the transeptal chapels, turned at a later date into
burial-places for two local families, are very large
and roomy. The cross-plan of Burford church in
Oxfordshire was formed in this way, early in the
thirteenth century. Plans like this, in which the
chapels grow out of the central space, instead of
being planned from the first in relation to it, are
imperfectly cruciform ; but are highly characteristic
of the irregular methods of development pursued by
the builders of medieval parish churches.

§ 65. Towers above transeptal chapels are not
uncommon. The two transeptal towers at Ottery
St Mary in Devon were doubtless copied from the
arrangement at Exeter cathedral : there was an altar
against the east wall of each chapel. The tower
at Coln St Aldwyn, Gloucestershire, rises above a
south chapel projecting from an aisleless nave. This

addition was made in the fifteenth century. At
Duddington in Northamptonshire the ground floor
of the tower virtually forms, in its present state, an
eastward extension of the south aisle parallel to the
western part of the chancel : the original plan was
probably similar to the present plan of Coln St
Aldwyn. The noble church of Whaplode had transeptal chapels projecting from the east end of either
aisle : the thirteenth century tower is above the
south chapel. At Clymping in Sussex the arrangement is very peculiar. The church, which is almost
entirely of the thirteenth century, has north and
south transeptal chapels, and only a south aisle to
the nave. The tower, which is at the end of the
south chapel, is earlier than the rest of the building,
but is clearly in its original position.

§ 66. The early progress of Gothic art in parish
churches was marked by a general lengthening of
chancels, analogous to that elongation of the eastern
arm which is characteristic of cathedrals and monastic
churches. This may be seen very clearly at Iffley,
near Oxford, and Avening in Gloucestershire, where
vaulted chancels of the twelfth century were lengthened in the thirteenth century by an eastern bay.
Sometimes, as at St Mary's, Shrewsbury, where
successive generations of builders were very faithful
to the remains of earlier work, the old sedilia of a
twelfth century chancel have been left in place.

But, as a rule, the enlargement of the chancel implied an entire reconstruction, or the entire transformation of old work by the insertion of new windows or buttresses. From the end of the twelfth century onwards, the normal chancel of the parish church has a length which is from a half to two-thirds of the length of the nave, the nave being slightly broader than the chancel. This is the case with most of those Norfolk churches, which may be regarded as the ideal examples of parish church planning. Room was in this way secured both for the altar and the quire stalls, for which the ordinary rectangular chancel offered a very restricted space.

§ 67. Sometimes a new chancel encroached upon the nave. This happened at Skipwith in Yorkshire, where the church underwent some alteration about the middle of the fourteenth century. The new chancel was made of the same width as the nave ; and apparently the old chancel arch was entirely removed, and its site, with the part of the nave immediately west of it, made into an extra bay of the chancel. No new chancel arch was built. One of the most curious and perplexing instances, in which additional westward room has been given to the chancel, and there is no structural division between chancel and nave, is at Tansor in Northants. The perplexity which arises here is due to the plentiful re-use of old work by the builders, the presence of

which in unexpected places makes the history of the
building a nearly insoluble puzzle. The church reached
its present length about 1140, when probably the
Saxon nave was left as the west part of a church,
which was now of the same width the whole way
through, and had no chancel arch. Some forty years
later, narrow aisles of three bays were added to the
nave ; and, about the same time, a transeptal chapel
may have been thrown out from the south wall,
immediately east of the south aisle. As the church
stands on southward sloping ground, there seems to
have been no room for another chapel on the north
side. In the thirteenth century, the aisles were
lengthened eastwards, to flank the western part of
the chancel. The builders moved back the eastern
responds of the old arcades to the points from which
the lengthened arcades were to start. They set
themselves, however, a difficult problem when they
reserved a space at the end of the north aisle for a
sacristy, and set the respond on the west side of this
narrow bay. Their north aisle thus consisted of five
bays and a very narrow eastern bay for the sacristy.
On the south side no space corresponding to the
sacristy was marked out, although the eastern respond
was placed in a line with the east side of the
opening of the sacristy. The number of bays on the
south side had to be five, as there was no room for
six. The result is that the pillars of the arcades, with

the exception of those of the two bays furthest west, which were left unaltered, are not opposite each other. In the meantime, the old transeptal chapel was left standing between a south aisle and a short south chapel of the chancel. About 1300, the aisle and chapel seem to have been widened to the full length of the transeptal chapel, and thus a broad south aisle was formed. In this plan, the chancel proper projects for some distance east of the aisles; but, for ritual purposes, the eastern part of the nave, corresponding to the eastern bay of the north aisle and the sacristy bay beyond, forms, and has formed since the twelfth century, a western extension of the chancel.

§ 68. The addition of aisles to chancels was an even more gradual process than the addition of aisles to naves; and, as a rule, the aisles were at first mere chapels. Chancel aisles or chapels of twelfth century date are not very common in smaller churches. But a plan like that at Melbourne, where the apsidal chapels east of the transepts flank the chancel very closely, leads naturally to the provision of chapels communicating directly with the chancel. The logical consequence of such a plan is seen at Oundle, at the close of the twelfth century, where rectangular chapels were built along the north and south walls of the western part of the chancel. The walls were pierced with broad, low arches, and arches were built between the chapels and the transepts. The chapels, in this instance, are at the back of the quire stalls ; and a long projecting piece of aisleless chancel was left beyond them, to which, in the fifteenth century, a large northern vestry was added. This plan, where both chancel chapels were added at much the same time and on the same scale, is symmetrical. But, as a rule, chancel chapels were built just when they were needed. At Arksey, near Doncaster, where, as at St Mary's, Shrewsbury, the walls of late twelfth century transepts have been largely preserved inside the church in spite of many alterations, the chancel is a long aisleless twelfth century building east of a central tower. Towards the end of the thirteenth century, the north chancel wall was pierced, and a narrow chapel built, which was one bay shorter than the chancel itself. In the fourteenth and fifteenth centuries the nave was enlarged, and the south aisle was widened to the full length of the south transept. A south chapel was added to the chancel : its outer wall was continued from the south wall of the transept, and carried eastwards for a little distance beyond the east wall of the chancel. Thus chancel, south chapel, and north chapel, are all of three different lengths and breadths, the south chapel being the longest and widest. When the south chapel was built, a considerable portion of the old chancel wall was left untouched on its north side. It is obvious that the methods of building employed in such additions were those which have been described in connexion with the addition of aisles to a nave. It is no uncommon thing to enter, as at Tamworth, a chancel aisle or chantry chapel, and find substantial remains of the old outer wall of the chancel, which has been pierced with one or more arches of communication.

§ 69. As the relative dates and proportions of chancel chapels vary so greatly, it is obvious that in many cases only one will be found. We frequently meet with churches which have only one aisle to the nave ; but these are for the most part small buildings, and one aisle usually, in larger buildings, presupposes another, although symmetry of proportion need not be expected. However, many important churches have one chancel chapel, and no more. Raunds in Northamptonshire, and Leverington in Cambridgeshire, have south, but not north, chapels. Stanion in Northamptonshire, and Hullavington in Wiltshire, have north, but not south chapels. In both these last cases, the chapels are simply continuations of the aisles, without a break or intermediate arch ; and the chapel at Stanion is neither more nor less than a second chancel. As the dedication of Stanion church is to St Peter and St Paul, it is not unlikely that the prominence given to the north chapel may be due to the provision of altars for both saints. The same consideration may have influenced the building of

the church at Wisbech, which is also dedicated to
St Peter and St Paul. Here, the twelfth century
chancel had a south chapel; but when, at the end
of the thirteenth century, the chancel was lengthened,
the south chapel was also enlarged into what is
practically a second chancel. Not only this, but the
south aisle of the church was rebuilt on the scale of a
second nave, a second south aisle was built out beyond
it, and the whole church, which afterwards was enlarged towards the north and otherwise altered, was
more than doubled in size.

§ 70. Where chantry chapels are attached to one
side or other of a chancel, their variations in size and
plan are almost infinite. In the smallest examples,
they are mere projections from the wall of the
chancel, and little more than tomb recesses, such as
the Cresacre chapel at Barnburgh, near Rotherham,
or the Booth chapel on the south side of the chancel
at Sawley in Derbyshire. The little north chapel
of the chancel at Clapton-in-Gordano in Somerset
may have served as a vestry. At Brancepeth, near
Durham, where there is a long chancel and an aisled
nave with transeptal chapels, a south chantry chapel
adjoins the east side of the south transeptal chapel,
while a north chantry chapel forms an independent
excrescence from the north wall, and is shut off from
the chancel by a doorway. Brigstock in Northamptonshire has a very large north chancel chapel,

which is virtually the eastern portion of a widened
aisle : the south chapel, on the other hand, is of much
later date, and is so small that there must have been
room in it for an altar and little more. These smaller
chantry chapels, like the beautiful south chapel at
Aldwinkle All Saints, Northants, have often great
architectural beauty of their own, and give great
variety to the plan of the church. But chancel
chapels are often larger and more important, like the
fourteenth century south chapel at Leverton, near
Boston, which is practically a separate building,
separated from the chancel by a wall without an
arcade, or like the very spacious north chapel of
the priory church at Brecon. The south chapel of
the chancel at Berkeley in Gloucestershire, and the
Clopton chapel at Long Melford in Suffolk, are shut
off from the adjacent parts of the church, and belong
to that class of chantry chapel of which our cathedrals
furnish many examples. In this case, the chapel is a
small separate building, attached to the fabric of the
church, but hardly forming an integral part of it.

§ 71. One very important consequence of the
addition of aisles and chantry chapels to chancels,
at any rate on a large scale, is seen where they are
applied to plans originally cruciform. We have
already seen that at St Mary's, Shrewsbury, and at
Arksey, although much of the fabric of the old transepts
was left, broad chancel chapels tended to obliterate

the cruciform character of the building. The transepts at Spalding almost escape notice, owing to the
double aisle on the south side of the nave, the aisle
and north chapel on the opposite side, and the large
chapel east of the south transept. Moreover, when,
in the fourteenth and fifteenth centuries, aisles were
rebuilt or widened, there was always, as at Tansor, a
tendency to decide the width of the aisle by the
length of an existing transept or transeptal chapel,
and to build the new outer wall flush with its gable
wall. In this case, the aisle would be planned to
communicate with the transept, and the west wall of
the transept would have to be cut through. Where,
as at Arksey, there was a central tower, the old
transept was structurally necessary, and only as
much of its masonry would be removed as was
absolutely necessary. But we have seen that there
were cases in which it was thought advisable to take
down the central tower altogether, and build a new
one at the west end, in which case the transepts
were of no structural use; and there were far more
cases in which the transeptal excrescences were merely
projecting chapels. In these instances, the transept
was felt to intervene awkwardly between the aisles
of nave and chancel. Accordingly, its side walls and
gabled roof were taken down, its end wall was
remodelled, and it was placed under one roof with
the adjacent aisles, in which it became merged.

The cruciform plan was thus lost in certain churches, becoming absorbed in the ordinary elongated plan, with aisles to nave and chancel. Tamworth church in Staffordshire, and Marshfield in Gloucestershire, had twelfth century central towers. These were removed or destroyed, at Tamworth in the fourteenth, at Marshfield in the fifteenth century, and the aisles and chancel chapels were widened to the original length, approximately, of the transepts. The north and south arches of the crossing, however, remain in a blocked condition, and tell the tale of what has happened. Wakefield cathedral is another instance of a large parish church whose aisleless cruciform plan has gradually disappeared within the aisles, until the plan is—or was till the additions of a few years ago—an aisled rectangle, the origin of which is certainly not obvious at first sight. The transformations here described must clearly be understood not to apply to cruciform churches generally, but merely to churches which, with an originally cruciform plan, needed enlargement. Many handsome late Gothic buildings, like the churches of Rotherham and Chesterfield, or St Mary's at Nottingham, are regular cruciform churches with central towers; and sometimes, as at Newark, transeptal chapels were the latest of all additions to a church. But, where the transeptal chapel cramped necessary space, it had to disappear. At St Margaret's, Leicester, the arches into the transeptal chapels remain; but the chapels themselves have entirely disappeared, and the arches merely form part of the arcade between the nave and its broad aisles.

§ 72. The aim of restorers and rebuilders from the middle of the fourteenth century onwards was to convert the church into a rectangle with aisles. As we have seen, the chancel was constantly, in late Gothic churches, an aisleless projection from the main fabric; but, where it was aisled, the old haphazard methods were often abandoned, and the aisles were made of approximately equal size. The old distinction between nave and chancel, marked by the chancel arch, and the arches between chapels and aisles, begin to vanish. Where the chancel arch was kept, as at Long Sutton in Lincolnshire, new chancel chapels were prolonged westward on each side of the nave, in place of the old nave aisles. Fairford church in Gloucestershire was rebuilt towards the end of the fifteenth century, to contain the splendid stained glass which had just been acquired for it. A central tower was built on strong piers, as a concession to the old plan ; but the aisles of the nave were continued on either side of the tower and along the sides of the chancel till within a bay of the east end. But, in a great many churches, not merely the aisles, but the nave and chancel also became continuous, without a structural division. This feature, common in East

Anglia and the south-west of England, was the result
of the importance of carved and painted wood-work
in late Gothic churches. The rood screen, stretching
across nave and aisles, appeared to full advantage,
when unbroken by the chancel arch. The splendid
timber roofs of nave and aisles gained in effect, if
they formed, as at Southwold, or in the churches of
Norwich, an unbroken covering to the church from
end to end. In Norfolk and Suffolk, where the work
of rebuilding began in the fourteenth century, as at
Cawston, Worstead, or Tunstead, the chancel arch was
often kept. At Worstead and other Norfolk churches
the method pursued by the builders was precisely
opposite to that which we have seen employed by
Gloucestershire masons at Cirencester and other
places, and may see in most of the fifteenth century
churches of Somerset. The arcades were rebuilt first,
and the aisles followed. Many of these churches were
doubtless enlarged from much smaller buildings. The
south aisle at Ingham was probably the nave of the
earlier church, to which the present nave, north aisle,
chancel, and west tower, were added. The aisles in
most cases continued at a uniform width eastward as
chancel chapels. The north aisle at Worstead was
continued by a two-storied sacristy to the level of the
east wall of the chancel. The south aisle stops at a bay
short of the east wall, leaving the end of the chancel
projecting as an altar space. Whether the chancel

arch was retained or not, the projection of this aisle-less eastern bay became a very general feature of the larger churches of East Anglia, and, in churches like Trunch, Southwold, and Clare, its tall side windows flood the space with light. The most striking example of this plan is at Long Melford in Suffolk, where there is no chancel arch, and the actual chancel projects beyond the aisles. Here, however, it is flanked on the north by the Clopton chapel, and on the south by the vestry, which forms a covered way to the detached lady chapel further east. The Long Melford plan, with a projecting altar space, and without a chancel arch, is nearly universal in Cornwall, and is common in south Devon, where, as at Totnes, the aisles of the chancel are usually little more than comparatively short chapels, and sometimes, as at West Alvington, near Kingsbridge, extend only a bay beyond the screen. Its great advantages, apart from the display of wood-work which it permits, are the gain of internal space permitted by the reduction of the solid portions of the building to a minimum, the additional light admitted by the same means, and the long uninter-rupted clerestory which forms a wall of glass, with thin stone divisions, on each side of the upper part of the church.

§ 73. The tendency to give the whole church aisles of equal width throughout, and extending along its whole length, was irresistible, especially in East

Anglia. The church of North Walsham, rebuilt towards the end of the fourteenth century, is a great rectangle of three parallel divisions, with axes from east to west, and of nearly equal breadth. The chapel of St Nicholas at Lynn, rebuilt in 1419, is an even more striking example of the same design: in both cases the simple and somewhat monotonous plan is varied by the projection of a handsome south porch. At Lynn, the thirteenth century west tower, with a spire, was kept at the south-west corner of the aisled building. But the aisled rectangular plan, if it attained its highest development in East Anglia, had been reached already in other parts of England by gradual methods. It has sometimes been fathered upon aisled naves of friary churches, which, like the great nave of the Black friars at Norwich, afforded space for large congregations who came to hear sermons. But it is probable that the first churches which followed the course of expansion into the aisled rectangle were directly influenced by the example of the larger churches, like Lincoln, or, at a later date, York, which, in extending their eastern arms, aisled their quires, presbyteries, and eastern chapels, right up to the east wall. Thus the whole quire and chancel of Newark, with aisles extending their whole length, were planned in the early part of the fourteenth century, when the great eastern chapel, the "Angel Quire," of Lincoln, was little more than a generation old; and, although the progress of the work was long delayed, the eventual arrangement, in which the high altar was brought two bays forward from the east wall, and a spacious chapel was left at the back, exactly recalls the arrangements of Lincoln and York. Similarly the quire and chancel of the cruciform church of Holy Trinity at Hull are aisled to their full length: the arrangement, again, is that of a cathedral rather than a parish church. The influence of cathedral plans is clearly visible in St Mary Redcliffe at Bristol, and in the collegiate churches of Ottery St Mary and Crediton: but here the type followed is not that of Lincoln and York, but that more usual in the west and south of England at Hereford, Wells, Salisbury, Exeter, and elsewhere, where the aisles of the chancel are returned at the back of the east wall. and form a vestibule to a projecting aisleless lady chapel. This type of plan occurs outside its regular district at Tickhill, on the borders of Yorkshire and Nottinghamshire. But it is naturally exceptional, and would be used only where there was plenty of money and space to spare: it demands for its full effect a considerable elevation, involving a large clerestory, and a church could seldom, if ever, be found whose original plan invited expansion on these lines. On the other hand, the aisling of the chancel throughout was simply the logical development of the ordinary church plan: if the plans of cathedrals may have suggested the later developments at churches like Newark or Hull, the simple aisled rectangle, with its three parallel divisions, and without any clerestory to distinguish the nave from the aisles—a plan remarkably characteristic of Cornwall—came into existence in the ordinary course of things, by an extension of the wings of the building until they flanked the whole of the nave and chancel.

§ 74. The work done at Grantham in the fourteenth and fifteenth centuries illustrates the purely natural development of the ordinary aisled church into the aisled rectangle. We have seen, in an earlier chapter, that, soon after 1300, the church consisted of an aisleless chancel, which was, however, overlapped at the west end by the north aisle of the nave; a nave, the north and south aisles of which followed different systems of spacing; a western tower and spire, engaged within the aisles; and north and south porches. Several chantries were founded in the church during the fourteenth century. Not long after the Black Death of 1349, the south aisle was extended eastward to the whole length of the chancel. The south wall of the chancel was pierced by an arcade; and the lady chapel thus formed was raised upon a double crypt. It was not until more than a century later that the east wall of the north aisle was taken down, and the "Corpus Christi chancel" built out, continuing the north aisle without a break, and completely flanking

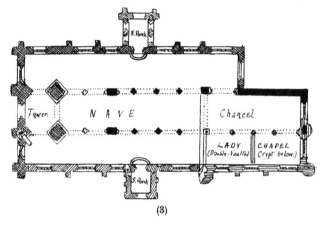

(3)

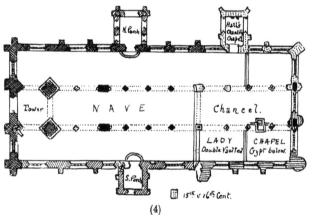

(4)

Fig. 16.   Plans of Grantham church :   (3) about 1350 ;
(4) present day.

the north wall of the chancel, through which an arcade was made. Here the reason of expansion was obviously the growth of chantry chapels; and the expansion follows the simplest course. The last addition to the fabric was the present vestry, in which was a chantry founded by the Hall family. This was built out at right angles to the north aisle, at the point where the old work was met by the later extension. Not until the church had been fully aisled, and afforded no further room for new altars, were chantry chapels usually added in the shape of excrescences from the fabric.

§ 75. One interesting feature in the planning of chancels, which has been much discussed, is worth a note. This is the fact that the axis of the chancel is frequently out of line with the axis of the nave, and generally has a slight northward inclination. Sometimes, as at Henbury in Gloucestershire, the inclination is very considerable, so that, from the west end of the church, nearly a quarter of the east wall is out of sight. Usually, the inclination is very slight ; and there are many cases in which it is not northward, but southward—Sidbury and Salcombe Regis, near Sidmouth, Eastbourne in Sussex and Aldwinkle St Peter in Northants, are cases in point. The popular explanation is that it symbolises the leaning of our Saviour's head upon the cross. Like most symbolical explanations, this is founded entirely upon fancy : the inclination is by no means confined to churches with cross plans, and, if it were, the theorists who argue from this standpoint confound the symbolism of the cross-plan between the cross itself and the Body which it bore. Others have sought to explain the phenomenon by suggesting that the orientation of the chancel followed the direction in which the sun rose on the morning of the patronal feast. A succession of visits at sunrise to churches on appropriate dates has not hitherto been attempted upon a comprehensive scale : if it were undertaken, it probably would· be found that the sun, instead of rising obediently opposite the middle light of every east window, as the theory requires, would have many puzzling exceptions in reserve. The marked divergence of axis at Henbury is explained by the site of the building, which is on a gentle slope, with the axis of the nave distinctly from south-east to north-west. When the chancel was rebuilt in the thirteenth century, the masons kept as high upon the slope as they could, and so twisted the axis of the chancel a little further east. But we must also remember that, when chancels were lengthened and rebuilt, the work was done while the old chancels were still standing. The axis of the old chancel might be out of line with that of the nave. Unless very careful measurements were taken, the new east wall would probably be not quite parallel with the old east wall of the chancel. The side walls would be set out at right angles to the new east wall ; and thus, when the new chancel was joined to the church, the divergence of axis would be more palpable than before. Or, for the same reason, a divergence of axis might be created for the first time. This seems to be the common sense explanation of a very common feature. But it must be added that there are instances in which the inclination is so decided that one is tempted to conclude either that the masons had very crooked sight, or that they were playing tricks with their perspective. The feature, where it is at all marked, is something of a deformity. In our own day it has been introduced, apparently by design, into the plan of Truro cathedral. In medieval work, however, it will seldom be found in a chancel where no enlargement upon an early site has taken place ; and it seems safe to conclude that, like so much else in medieval building which is irregular, it generally arises from the rebuilding of a fabric upon an encumbered site.

INDEX OF PLACES